BRUNCH
@ BOBBY'S

BRUNCH @ BOBBY'S

140 RECIPES FOR THE BEST PART OF THE WEEKEND

BOBBY FLAY

WITH STEPHANIE BANYAS & SALLY JACKSON

PHOTOGRAPHS BY BEN FINK

CLARKSON POTTER/PUBLISHERS
NEW YORK

Copyright © 2015 by Boy Meets Grill, Inc.

Photographs copyright © 2015 by Ben Fink

Published in the United States by
Clarkson Potter/Publishers, an imprint
of the Crown Publishing Group, a division
of Penguin Random House, LLC, New York.
www.crownpublishing.com
www.clarksonpotter.com

CLARKSON POTTER is a trademark and
POTTER with colophon is a registered
trademark of Penguin Random House LLC.

Library of Congress Cataloging-in-
Publication Data
Flay, Bobby, author.
  Brunch @ Bobby's / Bobby Flay with
Stephanie Banyas and Sally Jackson;
photographs by Ben Fink. —First edition.
    Includes index.
    1. Brunches. 2. Brunch @ Bobby's
(Television program) I. Banyas, Stephanie,
author. II. Jackson, Sally, 1978- author. III.
Title. IV. Title: Brunch at Bobby's.

  TX733.F58 2015
  641.5'2—dc23   2014012752

ISBN 978-0-385-34589-7
eISBN 978-0-385-34590-3

Printed in China

Book design by Danielle Deschenes
Cover design by Danielle Deschenes
Cover photography by Michael Crook
Stock cover photography: Shutterstock.com
© marekuliasz (chalkboard background)

10 9 8 7 6 5 4 3

First Edition

THANKS

As always, an extra special thank you to my two assistants and co-authors, Stephanie Banyas and Sally Jackson. Seven books together and counting . . . amazing!

A huge thank you to Christine Sanchez, Justin Hunt, Elyse Tirrell, and Lauren Bailey.

And thanks to everyone who played a big part in the creation of this cookbook:

BEN FINK

JEANNE LURVEY

DAHLIA WARNER

COURTNEY FUGLEIN

MICHAEL CROOK

BULLFROG & BAUM

IRIKA SLAVIN

FOOD NETWORK KOHL'S

KIM MARTIN

FRAN ALSWANG

REBECCA BREGMAN

ROCK SHRIMP
  PRODUCTIONS

MAGGIE JACKSON

MARYSARAH QUINN

DANIELLE DESCHENES

AMY BOORSTEIN

KIM TYNER

KATE TYLER

SARA KATZ

AARON WEHNER

DORIS COOPER

And, as always, Laurence Kretchmer.

Last but not least . . . the amazing Rica Allannic, the best editor in the business!

CONTENTS

INTRO

Brunch is my favorite meal of the week. I absolutely love it—and apparently I'm not alone. As I've traveled around America listening to all the enthusiastic eaters in this country, *Brunch* is the book you've asked me to write.

In New York, where I believe brunch was invented (I could be wrong, but it feels that way since I've lived here my whole life), restaurants are filled on the weekends with people drinking mimosas made with cheap sparkling wine and eating some version of eggs Benedict with overcooked poached eggs and neon-colored sauce from a box. They linger, reading the entire *New York Times* from cover to cover, as people hover over their tables, waiting for them to get up so that they can sit down and do the same exact thing.

People love brunch so much they are willing to endure the epic waits, the often so-so food and drinks, the hoverers. Now *that* I just don't get. Why not just invite your friends over and make it at home? The drinks won't be watered down, the food will be amazing, everyone will be comfortable, and you can keep the party going as long as you like.

You know I always kick things off with a cocktail—and brunch at my house is no exception. Often I set out a Bloody Mary Bar (page 32) so guests can customize their own, from the alcohol—gin or vodka—to the garnishes, which can go way beyond your typical celery. Or you can set out a pitcher of delicious, refreshing Blackberry-Bourbon Iced Tea (page 28). I also like to spice up the must-haves of coffee and tea by serving Spiked Iced Chicory Coffee (page 16) and Coconut Chai Tea Lattes (page 24). Fun drinks keep everyone entertained while I fry up a batch of light and airy Lemon Ricotta Fritters (page 169) with a sauce made from fresh raspberries. Everyone stands around my kitchen island, ready to pounce on the crisp yet fluffy fritters once they are out of the bubbling oil.

I am pretty detail oriented when it comes to brunch. I like a selection of breads, muffins, and sweet buns, such as Pumpkin-Cranberry Scones (page 177), Buttermilk Biscuits (page 154), and my favorite, Blackberry-Hazelnut Sticky Buns (page 158). That combination would make a great brunch bread basket, especially when paired with flavored butters, like Roasted Peach Butter (page 57) or Homemade Cinnamon-Sugar Butter (page 60), and interesting jams and preserves.

My brunch "musts" don't stop with a custom bread basket. Egg dishes must be cooked with care, sauces hand-whisked to velvety consistencies. If a "Benedict" is your go-to, try my crab cake version with Old Bay hollandaise on top of Johnnycakes (page 111), or take a trip to the south of Italy by serving up some Calabrian scrambled eggs on bruschetta (page 140). Pancakes should also be light and fluffy throughout with a subtle crust around the top edge. Carrot Cake Pancakes with Maple–Cream Cheese Drizzle (page 74) have become a cult favorite in my family. If waffles are your thing, Gingerbread Pumpkin Waffles with Buttermilk-Bourbon Caramel Sauce (page 89) take the classic to a new level.

Side dishes should never be an afterthought. Bacon should be crisp, of course, and it can even take on another flavor to balance out its intoxicating smokiness. Sometimes I glaze mine with maple and mustard (page 244) and guests ask me for the recipe over and over. They're always shocked at how easy it is! However, if you're going to make only one side dish to go with your eggs, you have to try Cast-Iron Home Fries with Roasted Green Chiles and Creamy Garlic Dressing (page 223). These potatoes are addictive and there's a chance they'll even steal the brunch show at your house.

Beyond the brunch classics, it's important to have in your arsenal a few dishes that lean more toward lunch than breakfast. Southern-inspired Fried Green Tomatoes with Shrimp Rémoulade (page 235) are just so satisfying; I love to serve them as a family-style platter. For an egg sandwich that's several notches up from your classic diner offering, make Country Ham and Fried Egg on Angel Biscuits (page 195). It's hard to stop at just one.

It's not quite breakfast and certainly not lunch. It's a special couple of hours that come only once a week. Brunch . . . savor it! And I look forward to seeing photos of all of your spectacular brunch dishes on Instagram, Facebook, and Twitter!

COFFEE,
TEA &
COCKTAILS

COFFEE MILK PUNCH

SERVES 6

A holiday tradition in the Deep South, milk punch is a creamy cocktail spiked with bourbon, vanilla, and occasionally spices. I like mine frozen until slushy and braced with coffee; chicory coffee, another southern staple, is a natural choice here.

3 cups whole milk

2 cups half-and-half

1 cup confectioners' sugar, sifted

1 teaspoon pure vanilla extract

1¼ cups bourbon

2 cups brewed coffee, preferably chicory coffee, cooled

⅛ teaspoon freshly grated nutmeg, plus more for serving

1 // Whisk together the milk, half-and-half, sugar, vanilla, bourbon, coffee, and nutmeg in a bowl. Cover and freeze until slushy, about 3 hours.

2 // Stir and serve in chilled glass mugs or tall glasses, topped with a grating of nutmeg.

ICED COFFEE

WITH CHILE DE ÁRBOL AND DARK CHOCOLATE

SERVES 2

Now *this* is how to jump-start your day! A step beyond your basic iced mocha, this coffee hits you with a thump of heat, thanks to the chile de árbol, which adds just enough fire to be thrilling, not painful.

1 cup whole milk

2 ounces bittersweet chocolate, chopped

2 tablespoons packed dark brown sugar, or more to taste

1 whole chile de árbol

3 cups brewed strong coffee

1 block bittersweet chocolate, for garnish, optional

1 // Combine the milk, chopped chocolate, sugar, and chile de árbol in a medium saucepan and bring to a simmer over low heat, stirring until the chocolate melts and the sugar dissolves. Add the coffee, remove from the heat, and let cool. Cover and refrigerate until cold, at least 2 hours and up to 1 day.

2 // Remove the chile before serving. Serve in tall glasses over ice. Grate chocolate on top, if desired.

SPIKED ICED CHICORY COFFEE

SERVES 4

Chicory is the roasted and ground root of the endive plant and has a rich, bittersweet flavor. Blended with coffee, as it has been in New Orleans since the coffee-pinching days of the Civil War, it makes for an especially rich, sweet cup. This spiked cocktail, iced with cubes made from the brew itself so as not to dilute its tremendous flavor, is a delicious way to toast a Big Easy brunch.

4 cups brewed chicory coffee, cooled

¼ cup half-and-half

6 tablespoons coffee liqueur, such as Kahlúa

¼ cup Simple Syrup (recipe follows)

1 // Pour 2 cups of the coffee into an ice cube tray and freeze until frozen, at least 2 hours or overnight.

2 // Combine the remaining 2 cups coffee, the half-and-half, liqueur, simple syrup, and the coffee ice cubes in a blender and blend until smooth. Pour into tall glasses.

SIMPLE SYRUP
MAKES ABOUT 1 CUP

1 cup sugar

Combine the sugar and 1 cup water in a small saucepan and bring to a boil over high heat. Cook until the sugar is dissolved, about 2 minutes. Remove from the heat and let the syrup cool. Cover and refrigerate until cold, at least 2 hours and up to 1 month.

SALTED CARAMEL AFFOGATO

SERVES 4

It's no secret that ice cream is my weakness, and "drowned" (that's the literal Italian translation of *affogato*) in piping hot, strong espresso . . . well, that's a brunch treat I happily endorse! The salt in the sweet gelato pulls all the other flavors into focus.

1 pint salted caramel gelato or ice cream (see Note)
2 cups brewed espresso, hot

Divide the ice cream among 4 glasses and pour the hot espresso on top. Serve immediately, with spoons and straws.

NOTE

If you can't find salted caramel gelato or ice cream, substitute regular caramel flavor ice cream and add a pinch of salt to the top of each affogato before serving.

MOROCCAN COFFEE GRANITA

AND ORANGE WATER CREAM PARFAITS

SERVES 4 TO 6

This deliciously spiced, Sambuca-splashed coffee granita looks great layered in tall glasses with orange-scented whipped cream. I like to serve this after a heavily spiced dish to help you cool off.

1½ cups espresso roast coffee beans

1 or 2 whole cloves, to taste

Seeds from 3 or 4 cardamom pods, to taste

1 tablespoon ground cinnamon

¼ teaspoon freshly grated nutmeg

¼ teaspoon ground ginger

¼ teaspoon freshly ground black pepper

½ cup granulated sugar

Splash of Sambuca

Orange Water Cream (recipe follows)

Candied orange peel, optional

Mint sprigs

1 // Working in batches if necessary, combine the coffee beans, cloves, cardamom seeds, cinnamon, nutmeg, ginger, and pepper in a coffee grinder and process until fine.

2 // Scoop the ground coffee into a coffee filter. Add 4 cups cold water and brew according to manufacturer's directions.

3 // Transfer the coffee to a small saucepan, add the sugar, and cook over low heat until the sugar is completely dissolved. Add the Sambuca and then pour the mixture into a 9 × 13-inch glass baking dish. Freeze until ice crystals begin to form around the edges, about 2 hours.

4 // Using a fork, stir the mixture well and return to the freezer. Continue freezing, stirring, and scraping every 30 minutes, until the mixture is thoroughly frozen and the crystals are fluffy, about 2 hours more. The granita can be kept overnight in the freezer.

5 // Layer the granita and orange water cream in tall glasses. Garnish with the candied orange peel, if desired, and mint sprigs.

ORANGE WATER CREAM
SERVES 4 TO 6

1 cup heavy cream, very cold

2 tablespoons confectioners' sugar

2 teaspoons orange flower water

1 teaspoon grated orange zest

¼ teaspoon pure vanilla extract

Combine all of the ingredients in the chilled bowl of a stand mixer fitted with the whisk attachment and whip until soft peaks form.

FROTHY HOT WHITE CHOCOLATE

SERVES 2

Smooth, rich, and creamy, this hot white chocolate gets its frothiness from a spin in the blender. Use a high-quality white chocolate, such as Valrhona, Lindt, or Callebaut; flavor and texture will suffer if you scrimp.

2 cups whole or skim milk (skim will froth better)

½ vanilla bean, split lengthwise and seeds scraped

1 tablespoon instant espresso powder

3 ounces best-quality white chocolate, coarsely chopped

Whipped cream

Unsweetened cocoa powder

1 // Combine the milk, vanilla bean and seeds, and espresso powder in a saucepan and bring to a simmer.

2 // Put the white chocolate in a blender and blend a few times to chop further. Remove the vanilla bean, pour the hot milk into the blender, and blend until frothy. Divide between 2 mugs, top with a dollop of whipped cream, and sprinkle with cocoa powder.

TEA LATTES

SERVES 4

There's no reason why coffee should get all the frothy milk fun—a brewed cup of black tea is just as deserving of special treatment. I particularly recommend giving Irish breakfast tea a try; its strong, slightly malty flavor is really brought to life when sweetened and served with milk.

4 Irish breakfast tea bags (or your favorite black tea)

2 tablespoons turbinado sugar, honey, or agave, or to taste

1 cup milk, either whole, 2%, or 1%

1 // Bring 3½ cups water to a boil in a small saucepan. Remove from the heat, add the tea bags and sugar, and let steep for 5 minutes. Discard the tea bags.

2 // While the tea is steeping, put the milk in a small saucepan and bring to a simmer. Use a handheld frother or whisk to froth the milk until foamy.

3 // Fill mugs halfway with the tea. Top with the frothy milk. Serve hot.

BERRY TEA SMOOTHIES

SERVES 4

Bright and citrusy red tea (I use Celestial Seasonings Red Zinger) is the base for this berry smoothie. I love the way it pumps up the fruity flavor and gorgeous red-pink hue without the calories found in juice, the usual choice. With just a touch of sweetener to taste, and just a bit of milk for creaminess, this smoothie is as it should be: totally delicious *and* good for you.

5 red tea bags

2 tablespoons sugar or honey, or to taste

1 (10-ounce) bag frozen mixed berries, thawed

¼ cup whole, 2%, or 1% milk, or half-and-half

1 // Pour 4 cups cold water into a medium saucepan and bring to a boil over high heat. Add the tea bags, remove from the heat, and let steep for 5 minutes. Discard the tea bags. Stir the sugar into the warm tea until it dissolves. Refrigerate until cold, at least 1 hour or overnight.

2 // Put the tea, berries, milk, and a few cups of ice in a blender and blend until smooth. Divide the drink among 4 tall glasses.

COCONUT CHAI
TEA LATTES

SERVES 4

You'll be amazed at just how simple it is to create your own version of this warm, spicy, sweet, and creamy teahouse (or coffee shop) specialty. Naturally, the real deal is so much better than most preblended commercial versions. I add coconut milk for its authentically Indian taste and the rich body it brings.

1 (2-inch) piece fresh ginger, thinly sliced

2 cinnamon sticks, plus more for serving

1 teaspoon black peppercorns

8 whole cloves

8 cardamom pods

6 black tea bags

1 cup whole or 2% milk

1 cup unsweetened regular or low-fat coconut milk

2 tablespoons to ¼ cup loosely packed light brown muscovado sugar, to taste

1 // Put the ginger in a medium saucepan. Lightly crush the cinnamon, peppercorns, cloves, and cardamom pods and add to the pan. Add 6 cups cold water and bring to a boil over high heat. Remove from the heat, cover, and let steep for 15 minutes.

2 // Return the mixture to the stove and bring back to a boil. Remove from the heat, add the tea bags, and let steep, covered, for 5 minutes.

3 // Put the milk, coconut milk, and sugar in a medium saucepan and bring to a simmer. Strain the tea mixture into the milk mixture, heat through for 1 minute, and then whisk until frothy. Pour into mugs, garnishing each with a cinnamon stick.

HIBISCUS TEA PUNCH

As colorful as it is tasty, this magenta-hued, refreshing, sangria-like punch will make any brunch gathering feel festive. If you can't find Pisco, a Peruvian grape brandy with a distinctive, complex flavor, substitute another clear fruit brandy or grappa.

3 hibiscus tea bags (I like Republic of Tea brand)

2 (750-ml) bottles Sauvignon Blanc

2 cups ruby red grapefruit juice

1¼ cups Pisco

½ cup Simple Syrup (page 16), or more to taste

1 small mango, peeled, pitted, and cut into small dice

1 small orange, halved and thinly sliced

1 cup raspberries or blackberries, or a mixture

1 // Bring 2¼ cups cold water to a boil in a small saucepan over high heat. Add the tea bags and let steep for 10 minutes. Remove the bags and discard.

2 // Pour the wine into a large container or pitcher. Add the tea, grapefruit juice, Pisco, simple syrup, half of the diced mango, and all of the orange slices. Cover and refrigerate for at least 4 hours or overnight.

3 // Just before serving, add the remaining diced mango and the berries. Serve over ice.

BLACKBERRY-BOURBON ICED TEA

SERVES 4 TO 6

I like to macerate sweet blackberries until they're extra juicy before adding them to black tea. Sure, you could serve this as is, strained and chilled over ice with mint, but why stop there? A shot of smoky bourbon floated on top makes this combination that much better.

3 cups fresh blackberries, plus more for serving

¾ cup sugar

2 tablespoons chopped fresh mint, plus whole sprigs for serving

6 good-quality black tea bags

Good-quality bourbon, such as Woodford Reserve

1 // Combine the blackberries and sugar in a large bowl and mash with a potato masher or wooden spoon.

2 // While the blackberries are macerating, bring 1½ quarts cold water to a boil in a medium saucepan over high heat. Remove from the heat, add the mint and tea bags, and let steep for 3 minutes. Remove the bags and pour the tea over the blackberry mixture. Let sit at room temperature for at least 1 hour and up to 4 hours for the flavors to meld.

3 // Pour the mixture through a strainer into a pitcher, pressing on the solids. Cover and refrigerate until cold, at least 2 hours or overnight.

4 // Serve over ice in tall glasses, floating a shot of bourbon on top of each and garnishing with some blackberries and the fresh mint sprigs.

BELLINI BAR

This Bellini bar is a fun and delicious way to get your guests involved in the merrymaking. The traditional Bellini, as first served up in Venice's Cipriani's, is a summery sweet concoction of Prosecco and white peach puree. Why not mix it up a little, with a selection of juicy fruit purees, liqueurs, and fresh garnishes? You don't need all of the ingredients listed, opposite; aim for some variety to make things interesting. Figure a couple of tablespoons of fruit puree per glass of sparkling wine, a dash of liqueur, and some fruit to garnish. Make it an all-American affair by serving a California sparkling wine as your base.

California Sparkling Wine
(or sparkling water for virgin drinks)

Fruit Puree

Passion Fruit Puree

Black Cherry Puree

Blueberry-Pomegranate Puree

Blackberry Puree

Peach Puree

Liqueur

Kirsch

Peach Eau de Vie

Chambord

Passion Fruit Liqueur

Fruit Garnish

Fresh Blackberries

Fresh Cherries

Pomegranate Seeds

Passion Fruit Seeds

BLOODY MARY BAR

What's the difference between a good Bloody Mary and a great one? I'd have to say it's a matter of taste and freshness. Nothing beats a totally customized Bloody Mary made to order. From the basics to the spike, the seasonings, and on down to the garnishes, there are a variety of directions you can take this classic brunch cocktail. Pick and choose your favorites within each heading, and let the fun begin!

Juice

Fresh Tomato Juice

V8 Juice

Clamato Juice

Liquor

Premium Vodka

Premium Tequila

Premium Gin

Seasoning

Worcestershire Sauce

Tabasco Sauce

Habanero Hot Sauce

Jalapeño Hot Sauce

Prepared Horseradish

Celery Salt

Old Bay Seasoning

Garnish

Fresh Lemons, Cut into Wedges

Celery Stalks

Jalapeño Chiles

Pickled Jalapeño Chiles

Pickled Onions

Pickled Asparagus Stalks

Pickled Okra

Black and Green Olives

Blue Cheese–Stuffed Olives

EARL GREY SPRITZER

Distinctively fragrant, Earl Grey tea saturates simple syrup with its citrusy bergamot essence. Cooled and poured over crisp Champagne, this elegant cocktail is tasty and aromatic.

¾ cup Earl Grey Syrup (recipe follows), cold

1 (750-ml) bottle Champagne or sparkling wine, very cold

4 thin slices of lemon

1 // Put 4 champagne flutes in the freezer at least 15 minutes before serving drinks and up to 24 hours.

2 // Remove the flutes from the freezer and divide the Earl Grey syrup among the glasses. Fill the glasses to the top with Champagne and garnish each with a lemon slice.

EARL GREY SYRUP
MAKES ABOUT 1 CUP

1 cup sugar

2 Earl Grey tea bags

Combine the sugar and 1 cup water in a small saucepan and bring to a boil over high heat. Cook until the sugar is dissolved, about 2 minutes. Remove from the heat, add the tea bags, and let steep for 10 minutes. Discard the tea bags and let the syrup cool. Cover and refrigerate until cold, at least 2 hours and up to 1 month.

MOJITO CHAMPAGNE COCKTAIL

SERVES 4

The addition of chilled sparkling wine (I prefer Spanish cava here) somehow makes this sweet mint and rum concoction perfectly appropriate for morning brunch. Should you find yourself with leftovers, the mint simple syrup is an excellent sweetener for iced tea.

½ cup white rum

¼ cup Mint Syrup (recipe follows)

Fresh mint leaves

1 (750-ml) bottle cava or other sparkling wine, cold

1 // Put 4 champagne flutes in the freezer at least 15 minutes before serving and up to 24 hours.

2 // Remove the flutes from the freezer and divide the rum and mint syrup among the glasses. Add a mint leaf to each. Fill the glasses to the top with cava.

MINT SYRUP
MAKES ABOUT 1 CUP

1 cup sugar

1 bunch fresh mint leaves

Combine the sugar and 1 cup water in a small saucepan and bring to a boil over high heat. Cook until the sugar is dissolved, about 2 minutes. Remove from the heat, add the mint leaves, and let steep for 30 minutes. Strain the syrup into a jar and let cool. Cover and refrigerate until cold, at least 2 hours and up to 1 month.

SANGRIA SUNRISE

SERVES 6 TO 8

I love a cold glass of sangria, the blend of fruits and their juices enhancing the wine's natural fruitiness. The traditional additions of brandy and Triple Sec make it a bit more potent—not exactly what I'm ready for on a Sunday morning! This sunrise-ready version, so called for the way the red wine bleeds down into the orange base, pumps up the juices in place of the liquors.

1 small pineapple

2 cups fresh orange juice, cold

2 cups fresh blackberries

1 small orange, halved and thinly sliced

1 lime, halved and thinly sliced

1 (750-ml) bottle fruity red wine

1 // Cut the top and bottom off the pineapple, stand it upright on a cutting board, and remove the peel using a sharp knife. Cut the pineapple into quarters lengthwise and then cut away and discard the tough core from each quarter. Finely dice enough of the pineapple to make 1 cup. Cut the remaining pineapple into chunks and put into a blender. Puree until smooth. Strain through a fine-mesh strainer, pressing on the solids; discard the solids. Measure 2 cups pineapple juice in a glass measuring pitcher; reserve any extra juice for another use.

2 // Combine the pineapple juice, orange juice, diced pineapple, blackberries, orange, and lime in a pitcher. Cover and refrigerate for at least 2 hours and up to 8 hours.

3 // Fill large wine goblets halfway with ice cubes and then top with the juice mixture and a splash of red wine.

BLOOD ORANGE CAMPARI MIMOSAS

SERVES 4

Garnet red and bubbly, this is one of the most spectacular-looking takes on the Mimosa I've ever seen. Sweet-tart, gorgeously hued blood orange juice gets an additional punch of color from a dash of Campari, a natural bittersweet pairing for citrus. This winter brunch cocktail is especially refreshing, not overly sweet.

1 cup blood orange juice

4 teaspoons Campari

1 (750-ml) bottle Champagne, Prosecco, or sparkling wine, cold

Thin slices of orange

Mint sprigs

1 // Put 4 champagne flutes in the freezer at least 15 minutes before serving and up to 24 hours.

2 // Remove the flutes from the freezer and divide the orange juice and Campari among the glasses. Fill the glasses to the top with Champagne. Garnish with the orange slices and mint sprigs.

WATERMELON MARGARITA MIMOSAS

SERVES 4

Sweet, juicy watermelon is one of summer's simplest pleasures, and a margarita made from its pink juice is one of my favorites. Simple syrup heightens the watermelon's natural sweetness and balances the lime juice's bright acidity. Crisp, sparkling cava joins the mix, making this margarita a brunch-bound Mimosa.

3 cups seedless watermelon cubes, cold

¼ cup fresh lime juice

¼ cup silver tequila

2 tablespoons Triple Sec

Simple Syrup (page 16), to taste

1 (750-ml) bottle cava or other sparkling wine, cold

1 // Put 4 champagne flutes in the freezer at least 15 minutes before serving and up to 24 hours.

2 // Put the watermelon in the blender and puree until smooth. Strain through a fine-mesh sieve, pressing on the solids; discard the solids. Measure 1 cup watermelon juice in a glass measuring pitcher; reserve any extra juice for another use.

3 // Add the lime juice, tequila, and Triple Sec to the pitcher and sweeten with simple syrup to taste.

4 // Remove the flutes from the freezer and divide the watermelon mixture among the glasses. Fill the glasses to the top with cava.

CARROT-MANGO MIMOSAS

SERVES 4

This is a fun brunch cocktail to pair with a healthy meal, something that once again proves that nutritious can be oh so delicious. Bright orange carrot juice, chock-full of antioxidants and vitamins, is naturally sweet, and mango juice amplifies that sweetness with a tropical flair.

½ cup mango nectar, cold

½ cup carrot juice, cold

1 (750-ml) bottle sparkling wine, cold

4 thin slices of mango

4 thin half-moon slices of orange

1 // Put 4 champagne flutes in the freezer at least 15 minutes before serving and up to 24 hours.

2 // Combine the mango nectar and carrot juice.

3 // Remove the flutes from the freezer and divide the juice mixture among the flutes. Fill the glasses to the top with sparkling wine and then garnish each glass with a thin slice of mango and orange.

TANGERINE-GIN FIZZ

SERVES 4

Freshly squeezed tangerine juice is like a quick shot of summery sunshine and such a winter treat. It's a lightly tart and refreshing twist on regular orange juice that pairs really nicely with herbal, juniper-scented gin. Top off the glasses with cold Champagne for a delightful brunch cocktail.

3 cups fresh tangerine juice

¾ cup best-quality gin

1 (750-ml) bottle cava, Champagne, or other sparkling wine, cold

4 orange slices, optional

1 // Put 4 champagne flutes in the freezer at least 15 minutes before serving and up to 24 hours.

2 // Remove the flutes from the freezer and divide the tangerine juice and gin among the glasses. Fill the glasses to the top with cava and garnish each with an orance slice, if desired.

RAMOS FIZZ

SERVES 1

An old-fashioned drink to be sure, the Ramos Fizz is yet another legendary recipe born in New Orleans. The milk and egg white (be sure to use only the freshest egg—or pasteurized, even—as it is served raw) combine during the shaking process into a luxuriously silky textured base for the botanical notes of gin, the tartness of lemon and lime juices, and the faint hint of orange flower water.

3 tablespoons gin

1 tablespoon fresh lemon juice

1 tablespoon fresh lime juice

2½ tablespoons Simple Syrup (page 16)

¼ cup skim or whole milk

1 small egg white, pasteurized, if desired

2 drops orange flower water

Club soda

In a cocktail shaker filled with ice, combine the gin, lemon juice, lime juice, simple syrup, milk, egg white, and orange flower water. Shake vigorously. Strain into a highball glass and top with club soda.

LA FRAISE

SERVES 4

A chunky puree of summer sweet strawberries, macerated with sugar, brought to life with lemon juice, and given depth with flecks of vanilla seeds, is the star of this pink cocktail. Strawberries are a classic accompaniment to Champagne, and I love the pairing in the glass itself. Delicious rosé Champagne, itself a lovely pink, is a fantastic choice for this beautiful cocktail inspired by the south of France.

½ pint fresh strawberries, preferably wild or fraises des bois, plus more for serving

2 tablespoons sugar, or more to taste

½ vanilla bean, split lengthwise and seeds scraped

1 teaspoon fresh lemon juice

1 (750-ml) bottle rosé Champagne, cold

1 // Combine the strawberries and sugar in a bowl and let sit at room temperature for 15 minutes. Mash using a potato masher or a fork into a chunky puree. Add the vanilla bean and seeds and the lemon juice. Cover and refrigerate for at least 1 hour or up to 4 hours. Discard the vanilla bean before serving.

2 // Put 4 champagne flutes in the freezer at least 15 minutes before serving and up to 24 hours.

3 // Remove the flutes from the freezer and put a tablespoon or two of the strawberry puree and the liquid into each flute. Fill the glasses to the top with Champagne and then garnish each with a strawberry.

SPREADS & SYRUPS

BLACKBERRY-MAPLE SYRUP

MAKES 1½ CUPS

This berry-laden maple syrup would be delicious poured over any plain waffle, pancake, or French toast. I call for blackberries because they are my personal favorite, but any berry would work.

1 pint fresh blackberries

1 cup pure grade B maple syrup

Combine the blackberries and maple syrup in a small saucepan, bring to a simmer over low heat, and cook, mashing gently with a wooden spoon, until the blackberries begin to break down slightly, about 5 minutes. Serve warm.

MAPLE BEURRE BLANC

MAKES ABOUT 1¼ CUPS

This is the best of both worlds—butter and syrup combined into one glorious sauce!

1 cup pure grade B maple syrup

8 tablespoons (1 stick) unsalted butter, cut into small pieces, cold

Pinch of fleur de sel or other coarse sea salt

Put the syrup in a small nonreactive saucepan over medium-low heat and bring to a simmer. Slowly whisk in the butter, piece by piece, until emulsified. Remove from the heat and season with the salt. Use immediately.

ALMOND BUTTER SYRUP

MAKES ABOUT 1 CUP

This nutty, rich sauce is perfect for Almond Croissant French Toast (page 94).

4 tablespoons (½ stick) unsalted butter
¼ cup sliced almonds
¾ cup pure grade B maple syrup
¼ teaspoon pure almond extract

Melt the butter in a small sauté pan over medium heat until it begins to shimmer. Add the almonds and sauté until lightly golden brown, 2 minutes. Add the syrup and almond extract and cook until heated through, a minute or two. Serve warm.

SALTED CARAMEL SAUCE

MAKES ¾ CUP

A perfect match for Double Chocolate Pancakes (page 68), this sauce is also amazing over a scoop (or two) of vanilla ice cream.

1 cup sugar
½ cup heavy cream
2 tablespoons unsalted butter, at room temperature
¾ teaspoon fleur de sel or other coarse sea salt

1 // Combine the sugar and ¼ cup cold water in a medium saucepan over high heat. Cook, without stirring or touching, until the sugar turns a deep amber color, 8 to 10 minutes.

2 // Meanwhile, warm the cream in a small saucepan or in the microwave. When the caramel is ready, slowly whisk in the cream and continue simmering until the mixture is smooth, about 2 minutes. Remove from the heat and stir in the butter and salt until combined. Serve warm.

BUTTERMILK-BOURBON CARAMEL SAUCE

MAKES ¾ CUP

Bourbon adds a nice smokiness to this caramel sauce, while tangy buttermilk keeps the sweetness level in check. Created for Gingerbread Pumpkin Waffles (page 89), this sauce—based on two of my favorite ingredients—is like a southern dulce de leche.

1¼ cups sugar

1 cup buttermilk

6 tablespoons (¾ stick) unsalted butter, quartered

2 tablespoons corn syrup

1 teaspoon baking soda

1 teaspoon pure vanilla extract

2 tablespoons bourbon or dark rum

Pinch of fleur de sel or other coarse sea salt

1 // Combine the sugar, buttermilk, butter, corn syrup, and baking soda in a medium saucepan and simmer over medium-high heat, whisking occasionally, until amber brown and slightly thickened, about 20 minutes.

2 // Remove from the heat and stir in the vanilla, bourbon, and salt. Serve warm.

MIXED BERRY SAUCE

MAKES 1¾ CUPS

I love berries—all berries—and this sauce is delicious (not to mention so easy to make) served alongside Lemon Ricotta Fritters (page 169) or Beignets (page 165).

1 (16-ounce) bag frozen mixed berries, thawed

¼ cup sugar

2 heaping tablespoons seedless raspberry preserves

1 tablespoon fresh lemon juice

1 // Combine the berries, sugar, and ¼ cup water in a medium saucepan. Bring to a boil over high heat and cook, stirring occasionally, until the berries are soft, about 10 minutes. Remove from the heat and let cool for 5 minutes.

2 // Transfer the berry mixture to a blender or food processor, add the raspberry preserves and lemon juice, and blend until smooth. Transfer to a bowl and let cool to room temperature. The sauce will keep, covered in the refrigerator, for up to 1 week.

QUICK HOMEMADE BERRY JAM

MAKES ABOUT 2 CUPS

It is possible to enjoy homemade jam without worrying about canning or waiting! This jam, delicious with Lemon Ricotta Fritters (page 169), is ready in no time.

1 quart ripe strawberries, blackberries, or raspberries, hulled

½ cup superfine sugar

2 tablespoons fresh lemon juice

Put the strawberries in a food processor and process until coarsely chopped. Transfer to a large skillet and stir in the sugar and lemon juice. Bring to a boil over medium-high heat, stirring occasionally, and cook until the jam is thickened, about 10 minutes. Transfer to a bowl and let cool to room temperature. The jam can be covered and refrigerated for up to 2 weeks.

ORANGE SYRUP

Freshly squeezed orange juice, enriched and enhanced with butter and orange liqueur, is cooked down with sugar to a sweet glossy sauce that, when combined with plump segments of the fruit, brings a shot of sunshine to any plate. Really want to pump up the orange appeal? Serve with Brûléed Orange French Toast (page 98) or for the suggested topping on Orange Ricotta Pancakes (page 76).

3 oranges

¾ cup sugar

2 tablespoons unsalted butter, cold

1 teaspoon orange liqueur, such as Grand Marnier

1 // Grate 1 teaspoon orange zest and reserve. Remove the segments from 2 of the oranges: slice off the tops and bottoms, stand the fruit on a cut side, and slice away the peel, pith, and a sliver of flesh. Working over a bowl and holding the fruit in one hand, run a paring knife between each orange segment and the membrane to free the segments. Collect the segments in the bowl. Squeeze out the membranes to remove as much juice as possible and discard the membranes. Set a strainer over a measuring cup and dump the segments into the strainer. Juice the remaining orange to make ½ cup juice. Reserve the juice and segments separately.

2 // Combine the sugar and ¼ cup water in a medium high-sided sauté pan over high heat and cook without stirring until caramelized, about 7 minutes. Carefully whisk in the orange juice, butter, and orange liqueur until melted and slightly thickened. Stir in the orange segments and zest and serve warm.

ORANGE-BLUEBERRY MARMALADE

MAKES ABOUT 4 CUPS

True English marmalade walks a delicate line between sweet and bitter, and this more-sweet-than-bitter blueberry version is amazing with hot Crumpets (page 150) or a slice of buttered toast.

4 medium oranges

2 lemons

1 cup fresh blueberries

3 cups sugar

1 (3-ounce) pouch liquid fruit pectin

1 // Using a vegetable peeler, remove the zest of the oranges and lemons, avoiding as much of the white pith as possible. Cut the zest into thin slices and then finely chop.

2 // Peel the remaining soft white pith from the fruit and discard. Chop the fruit pulp, reserving any juice and discarding the seeds.

3 // Combine the zest and 1½ cups cold water in a medium saucepan over high heat and bring to a boil. Reduce the heat, cover, and simmer, stirring occasionally, for 20 minutes. Add the fruit pulp and juice, cover, and simmer over low heat for an additional 7 minutes. Add the blueberries and simmer for 3 more minutes.

4 // Stir the sugar into the fruit in the saucepan. Bring the mixture to a full rolling boil over high heat and cook, stirring constantly, for exactly 1 minute. Stir in the pectin. Remove from the heat and skim off any foam with a metal spoon.

5 // Let cool and then cover and refrigerate. The marmalade will keep for up to 2 weeks.

CHUNKY GRANNY SMITH APPLESAUCE

MAKES 2 CUPS

This just-sweet-enough applesauce is a natural with Potato Pancakes (page 224) but is also great with a pork roast, or on its own as a snack.

Grated zest of 1 lemon

5 Granny Smith apples, peeled, cored, and diced

3 to 6 tablespoons sugar, to taste

2 cinnamon sticks

¼ teaspoon ground ginger

1 // Bring 1 cup water and the lemon zest to a boil over medium heat. Add the apples, 3 tablespoons of the sugar, the cinnamon sticks, and the ginger and cook until soft, 15 minutes.

2 // Taste for sweetness and add more sugar if desired. Coarsely mash to a chunky consistency. Let cool to room temperature. Remove the cinnamon sticks. The applesauce will keep, covered in the refrigerator, for up to 2 days.

WHIPPED BUTTER

MAKES 2 CUPS

There is nothing fresher than making your own butter. You can control just how much salt, if any, you'd like to use, and all you need is heavy cream and some arm (or mixer) power.

1 cup heavy cream, cold

Pinch of fine sea salt

1 // Freeze the bowl of a stand mixer until cold, at least 10 minutes.

2 // Combine the cream and salt in the cold bowl and attach the whisk attachment. Whip on low speed until the mixture begins to thicken, then increase the speed, and whip until light and fluffy and the mixture has turned into butter. Do not overmix or it will break. Scrape into a bowl and chill for at least 15 minutes before serving and up to 24 hours.

WHIPPED MAPLE BUTTER

Add ¼ cup pure grade B maple syrup to the cream and salt.

FRUIT BUTTERS

MAKES 1¼ CUPS

These are a really easy way to add extra flavor to toast, muffins, biscuits, pancakes, and waffles.

½ pound (2 sticks) unsalted butter, at room temperature

¼ cup fruit preserves, such as cherry, raspberry, strawberry, peach, or apricot

⅛ teaspoon kosher salt

Stir together the butter, preserves, and salt in a bowl until combined. Cover and refrigerate for at least 1 hour or up to 2 days to allow the flavors to meld. Let sit at room temperature for 15 minutes before serving.

ROASTED PEACH BUTTER

MAKES ABOUT 1½ CUPS

This is a delicious way to celebrate the best summer has to offer, especially when paired with Zucchini Pancakes (page 73).

2 ripe peaches, halved and pitted

Canola oil

2 tablespoons sugar

2 tablespoons peach eau de vie or schnapps

½ pound (2 sticks) unsalted butter, at room temperature

Pinch of fine sea salt

1 // Preheat the oven to 375°F.

2 // Brush the cut side of the peaches with a little oil and sprinkle with the sugar. Put the peaches, cut side up, on a baking sheet and roast until caramelized and very soft, about 30 minutes. Remove from the oven and let cool slightly.

3 // Peel the peaches and discard the skins. Put the peaches in a food processor, add the eau de vie, and puree until smooth. Add the butter and salt and puree until smooth. Scrape into a large ramekin, cover, and refrigerate for at least 1 hour and up to 24 hours to allow the flavors to meld. Bring to room temperature before using.

BOURBON MOLASSES BUTTER

MAKES ABOUT 1¼ CUPS

An homage to the flavors of the South, this butter makes a great topping for Silver Dollar Buttermilk-Pecan Pancakes (page 71).

½ cup good-quality bourbon

1 tablespoon sugar

12 tablespoons (1½ sticks) unsalted butter, at room temperature

3 tablespoons molasses

Pinch of fine sea salt

1 // Combine the bourbon and sugar in a small saucepan and bring to a boil over high heat. Cook until reduced by half, about 5 minutes. Set aside to cool.

2 // Put the butter, molasses, salt, and bourbon mixture in a food processor and process until smooth. Scrape into a bowl, cover with plastic wrap, and refrigerate for at least 1 hour to allow the flavors to meld and up to 8 hours. Remove from the refrigerator about 30 minutes before using to soften.

VANILLA BEAN BUTTER

MAKES ½ CUP

Flecked with specks of real vanilla bean and full of flavor, this butter is an elegant topping to Pain Perdu with Fresh Peaches (page 99).

8 tablespoons (1 stick) unsalted butter, at room temperature

1 tablespoon sugar

1 vanilla bean, split lengthwise and seeds scraped

Pinch of fine sea salt

Stir together the butter, sugar, vanilla seeds, and salt in a small bowl until combined. Cover with plastic wrap and refrigerate for at least 1 hour to allow the flavors to meld and up to 8 hours. Remove from the refrigerator about 30 minutes before using to soften.

HOMEMADE CINNAMON-SUGAR BUTTER

MAKES ABOUT 2 CUPS

One of my favorite childhood treats was cinnamon-sugar toast, and this compound butter delivers all that deliciousness to whatever it tops, especially Belgian Waffles (page 90).

1 cup heavy cream

Pinch of fine sea salt

3 tablespoons sugar

2 teaspoons ground cinnamon

Combine the cream and salt in a stand mixer fitted with the whisk attachment and beat until it becomes whipped butter. Combine the sugar and cinnamon in a small bowl and fold into the butter. Scrape into a bowl and mix until combined. Serve immediately or cover and refrigerate for up to 2 days. Remove from the refrigerator 30 minutes before serving.

WHIPPED CREAM CHEESE

MAKES ABOUT 3 CUPS

This lightly orange-scented whipped cream–cream cheese topping is delightful on Bananas Foster French Toast (page 97), and adds a tangy richness to any pancakes, French toast, or waffles you might otherwise top with plain whipped cream.

3 ounces cream cheese, at room temperature

1 teaspoon pure vanilla extract

½ teaspoon grated orange zest

1 cup heavy cream, cold

Put the cream cheese, vanilla, and orange zest in the bowl of a stand mixer fitted with the whisk attachment and whip until light and fluffy. Add the cream and whip until soft peaks form. Cover and refrigerate until ready to use.

FRESH DILL CREAM CHEESE

MAKES ABOUT 1 CUP

This is perfect on bagels or stirred into scrambled eggs.

8 ounces cream cheese, at room temperature

¼ cup finely chopped fresh dill

2 tablespoons dill pickle juice

Pinch of fine sea salt

Pinch of freshly ground black pepper

Stir together the cream cheese, dill, pickle juice, salt, and pepper in a bowl until smooth. Cover and refrigerate for at least 1 hour and up to 8 hours to allow the flavors to meld.

ROASTED JALAPEÑO– CILANTRO CREAM CHEESE

MAKES 1 CUP

I love bagels or toasted whole-grain breads for brunch and, while I don't make my own (there are so many great bakeries near me), I do like to add my own special touch by preparing homemade spreads to serve on top. Flavored cream cheeses are easy to make and taste so much fresher than store-bought.

8 ounces cream cheese, at room temperature

2 tablespoons milk

Kosher salt and freshly ground black pepper

2 jalapeño chiles, roasted (see page 116), peeled, seeded, and finely diced

¼ cup finely chopped fresh cilantro

Combine the cream cheese, milk, and salt and pepper to taste in a food processor and process until smooth and fluffy. Scrape into a bowl and fold in the jalapeños and cilantro. Cover and refrigerate for at least 1 hour or up to 24 hours to allow the flavors to meld. Let sit at room temperature for 30 minutes before serving.

HERBED GOAT CREAM CHEESE

Add 2 ounces fresh goat cheese and substitute ¼ cup thinly sliced green onions (white and green parts) and ¼ cup finely chopped fresh dill for the jalapeños and cilantro.

PANCAKES,
WAFFLES
& FRENCH
TOAST

SPICE RAISIN PANCAKES
WITH RUM RAISIN-CREAM CHEESE GLAZE

SERVES 4 OR 5; MAKES 12 TO 15 PANCAKES

These sweetly spiced pancakes—inspired by hot cross buns—will fill your kitchen with the warm scents of cinnamon, nutmeg, and cardamom.

¼ cup raisins

½ cup dark rum

¼ cup orange juice

1½ cups all-purpose flour

2 tablespoons light brown muscovado sugar

½ teaspoon ground cinnamon

¼ teaspoon ground cardamom

⅛ teaspoon freshly grated nutmeg

1 teaspoon baking powder

½ teaspoon baking soda

½ teaspoon fine sea salt

1½ cups buttermilk

3 tablespoons unsalted butter, melted, plus more for the griddle

2 large eggs

¾ teaspoon pure vanilla extract

1 tablespoon grated orange zest

3 ounces cream cheese, at room temperature

1 cup confectioners' sugar

Pure grade B maple syrup or honey, optional

1 // Combine the raisins, rum, and orange juice in a small saucepan and bring to a simmer over high heat. Remove from the heat and let sit for 15 minutes. Drain the raisins and reserve them and the soaking liquid separately.

2 // Whisk together the flour, muscovado sugar, cinnamon, cardamom, nutmeg, baking powder, baking soda, and salt in a medium bowl. Whisk together the buttermilk, butter, eggs, ½ teaspoon of the vanilla, and the orange zest in a small bowl. Add to the flour mixture and mix until just combined. Fold in the raisins. Cover and refrigerate for at least 1 hour and up to 4 hours.

3 // Preheat the oven to 250°F. Line a baking sheet with parchment.

4 // Beat together the cream cheese, confectioners' sugar, and remaining ¼ teaspoon vanilla until smooth. Thin out with some of the raisin soaking liquid to make a glaze.

5 // Heat a large cast-iron griddle or nonstick sauté pan over medium heat. Brush with butter and continue heating until the butter begins to foam. Drop scant ¼ cupfuls of batter onto the griddle. Bake until bubbles start to form and burst, about 2 minutes. Flip and cook to set the other side, another 1 to 2 minutes. As the pancakes are ready, put them in a single layer on the baking sheet and keep warm in the oven until ready to serve.

6 // Stack 3 pancakes per person, drizzle with cream cheese glaze, and top with maple syrup, if desired.

DOUBLE CHOCOLATE PANCAKES
WITH SALTED CARAMEL SAUCE

SERVES 4 OR 5; MAKES 12 TO 15 PANCAKES

The perfect way to spoil the chocolate lover in your life, these pancakes are undeniably decadent. My daughter and her friends used to beg for chocolate chip pancakes after sleepovers, and if you're going to cave, you might as well go all out! Big flakes of sea salt add a nice crunch of saltiness to the caramel and temper the dish's sweetness.

2 large eggs

1 tablespoon granulated sugar

2 tablespoons dark brown sugar

1¼ cups buttermilk, at room temperature

3 tablespoons unsalted butter, melted, plus more for the griddle

1 teaspoon pure vanilla extract

1½ cups all-purpose flour

¼ cup unsweetened cocoa powder

1 teaspoon instant espresso powder

2 teaspoons baking powder

¼ teaspoon fine sea salt

3 ounces semisweet or bittersweet chocolate, finely chopped

Salted Caramel Sauce (page 50), warm

Confectioner's sugar; optional

Raspberries; optional

1 // Whisk together the eggs, both kinds of sugar, buttermilk, butter, and vanilla in a small bowl until smooth. Whisk together the flour, cocoa powder, espresso powder, baking powder, and salt in a medium bowl. Add the egg mixture and whisk until just combined. Fold in the chocolate, cover, and let rest for 15 minutes.

2 // Preheat the oven to 250°F. Line a baking sheet with parchment.

3 // Heat a large cast-iron griddle or nonstick sauté pan over medium heat. Brush with butter and continue heating until the butter begins to foam. Drop scant ¼ cupfuls of batter onto the griddle. Bake until bubbles start to form and burst, about 2 minutes. Flip and cook to set the other side, another 1 to 2 minutes. As the pancakes are ready, put them in a single layer on the baking sheet and keep warm in the oven until ready to serve.

4 // Stack the pancakes on plates, drizzle with the warm caramel sauce, and top with a sprinkling of confectioners' sugar and some raspberries, if desired.

SILVER DOLLAR BUTTERMILK-PECAN PANCAKES

WITH BOURBON MOLASSES BUTTER

SERVES 4 TO 6; MAKES 24 TO 36
SILVER DOLLAR PANCAKES

Buttery pecans add a mild, nutty crunch to these light-as-can-be pancakes. Paired with the deep, almost smoky flavor of a bourbon molasses butter, it's like having pecan pie for brunch. Cooking the pancakes silver dollar size is optional, but there's just something so fun and appealing about a tall stack of silver dollar pancakes.

½ vanilla bean, split lengthwise, seeds scraped

1 teaspoon pure vanilla extract

2 large eggs

1½ cups plus 3 tablespoons buttermilk

3 tablespoons unsalted butter, melted, plus more for the griddle

1½ cups all-purpose flour

½ cup finely chopped toasted pecans, plus coarsely chopped pecans for serving

2 tablespoons granulated sugar

1 tablespoon light brown sugar

1 teaspoon baking powder

½ teaspoon baking soda

¾ teaspoon fine sea salt

Bourbon Molasses Butter (page 58)

Pure grade B maple syrup, warm

1 // Combine the vanilla seeds and vanilla extract in a small bowl. Whisk in the eggs, buttermilk, and butter.

2 // Whisk together the flour, finely chopped pecans, both types of sugar, baking powder, baking soda, and salt in a medium bowl. Whisk in the egg mixture until just combined. Do not overmix. Let sit at room temperature for 30 minutes or in the refrigerator for up to 1 hour.

3 // Preheat the oven to 250°F. Line a baking sheet with parchment.

4 // Heat a large cast-iron griddle or nonstick sauté pan over medium heat. Brush with butter and continue heating until the butter begins to foam. Drop 2 tablespoons of batter per pancake onto the griddle. Bake until bubbles start to form and burst, about 2 minutes. Flip and cook to set the other side, another 1 to 2 minutes. As the pancakes are ready, put them in a single layer on the baking sheet and keep warm in the oven until ready to serve.

5 // Stack 6 pancakes per person, topping each stack with some of the bourbon butter. Drizzle with warm maple syrup and garnish with coarsely chopped pecans.

OATMEAL COOKIE PANCAKES

WITH BANANAS AND MIXED BERRY SYRUP

SERVES 4; MAKES ABOUT 14 PANCAKES

Yes, you can start your day with a cookie and still feel somewhat virtuous! Hearty oats add body without weight to these delicious pancakes, and cinnamon, nutmeg, and of course a touch of brown sugar really do make them taste like the classic cookie treat. Sliced bananas and a maple syrup–sweet berry sauce add just the right all-American finishing touches.

1½ cups all-purpose flour

½ cup plus 1 tablespoon old-fashioned oats

2 teaspoons baking powder

1 teaspoon baking soda

¼ teaspoon fine sea salt

¾ teaspoon ground cinnamon

⅛ teaspoon freshly grated nutmeg

2 large eggs

2 tablespoons light brown muscovado sugar

¾ cup plus 1 tablespoon pure grade B maple syrup

2 cups buttermilk, plus more if needed

4 tablespoons (½ stick) unsalted butter, melted, plus more for the griddle

½ teaspoon pure vanilla extract

½ cup mixed berries, such as blueberries, raspberries, and blackberries

1 ripe banana, thinly sliced

Confectioners' sugar

1 // Whisk together the flour, oats, baking powder, baking soda, salt, cinnamon, and nutmeg in a large bowl. Whisk together the eggs, muscovado sugar, and 1 tablespoon of the maple syrup in a medium bowl until smooth. Add the buttermilk, butter, and vanilla and whisk until combined. Add to the flour mixture and whisk until just combined. Cover and refrigerate for at least 30 minutes and up to 3 hours. Whisk in a few extra tablespoons of buttermilk if needed to loosen the batter before cooking.

2 // Preheat the oven to 250°F. Line a baking sheet with parchment.

3 // Bring the remaining ¾ cup maple syrup to a simmer in a saucepan over low heat, add the berries, and cook until the berries soften slightly, about 2 minutes. Keep warm until ready to use.

4 // Heat a large cast-iron griddle or nonstick sauté pan over medium heat. Brush with butter and continue heating until the butter begins to foam. Drop scant ¼ cupfuls of batter onto the griddle. Bake until bubbles start to form and burst, about 2 minutes. Flip and cook to set the other side, another 1 to 2 minutes. As the pancakes are ready, put them in a single layer on the baking sheet and keep warm in the oven until ready to serve.

5 // Stack the pancakes on plates and top with the banana slices and some of the warm berries and syrup. Dust with confectioners' sugar.

ZUCCHINI PANCAKES

WITH ROASTED PEACH BUTTER
AND MAPLE SYRUP

SERVES 4 TO 6

A celebration of late summer's bounty, this is a plate of pancakes to feel good about. Zucchini adds tons of moisture to these light, fluffy pancakes, a riff on zucchini quick bread. Roasting peaches heightens their natural sweetness; blended with creamy butter and just a touch of peach liqueur, they make a rich, flavorful spread that coats each bite with the sweet taste of summer.

2 large eggs

3 tablespoons canola oil

1 tablespoon granulated sugar

2 tablespoons light brown muscovado sugar

¼ cup buttermilk

1 teaspoon pure vanilla extract

1 teaspoon grated orange zest

½ pound zucchini, shredded (about 2 cups), patted dry on paper towels

½ cup whole-wheat flour

½ cup all-purpose flour

1 teaspoon baking soda

1 teaspoon ground cinnamon

¼ teaspoon fine sea salt

Unsalted butter, for the griddle

Roasted Peach Butter (page 57)

Pure grade B maple syrup, warm

½ cup walnuts, toasted and coarsely chopped

1 // Preheat the oven to 250°F. Line a baking sheet with parchment.

2 // In a medium bowl, whisk together the eggs, oil, both types of sugar, buttermilk, vanilla, and orange zest until smooth; stir in the zucchini. In a large bowl, whisk together both types of flour, baking soda, cinnamon, and salt until combined. Add the egg mixture and mix until just combined. Do not overmix.

3 // Heat a large cast-iron griddle or nonstick sauté pan over medium heat. Brush with butter and continue heating until the butter begins to foam. Drop scant ⅓ cupfuls of batter onto the griddle. Bake until bubbles start to form and burst, 3 to 4 minutes. Flip and cook to set the other side, about 2 minutes. As the pancakes are ready, put them in a single layer on the baking sheet and keep warm in the oven until ready to serve.

4 // Stack 3 pancakes per person, spread with peach butter, and top with warm syrup and walnuts.

CARROT CAKE PANCAKES
WITH MAPLE-CREAM CHEESE DRIZZLE

SERVES 4; MAKES ABOUT 14 PANCAKES

These pancakes are light, fluffy, and chock-full of the flavors that make carrot cake so delicious—including pumpkin pie spice (a mix of cinnamon, ginger, nutmeg, and allspice), sweet candied ginger, toasted nuts, and orange zest—all without being too sweet. One of my favorite parts of carrot cake has to be the cream cheese frosting, and this smooth blend of cream cheese and maple syrup is the icing on the pancake!

1½ cups all-purpose flour

¼ cup sugar

1 teaspoon baking powder

½ teaspoon baking soda

1 teaspoon pumpkin pie spice

½ teaspoon fine sea salt

2 large eggs

1½ cups buttermilk

3 tablespoons unsalted butter, melted, plus more for the griddle

½ teaspoon pure vanilla extract

1 cup loosely packed finely grated peeled carrots, patted dry on paper towels (about 3 medium)

1 teaspoon grated orange zest

¼ cup finely diced candied ginger

¼ cup finely chopped toasted pecans or walnuts, plus coarsely chopped nuts for serving

3 ounces cream cheese, at room temperature

1 cup pure grade B maple syrup

1 // Whisk together the flour, sugar, baking powder, baking soda, pumpkin pie spice, and salt in a large bowl. Whisk together the eggs, buttermilk, butter, vanilla, carrots, and orange zest in a large bowl until smooth. Add to the flour mixture, fold in the ginger and finely chopped pecans, and mix with a rubber spatula until just combined. Cover and refrigerate for 30 minutes.

2 // Preheat the oven to 250°F. Line a baking sheet with parchment.

3 // Combine the cream cheese and maple syrup in the bowl of a stand mixer fitted with the whisk attachment and whip until combined, about 1 minute. Transfer to a heatproof bowl and then pop in the oven until just warmed through and easy to drizzle.

4 // Heat a large cast-iron griddle or nonstick sauté pan over medium heat. Brush with butter and continue heating until the butter begins to foam. Drop scant ¼ cupfuls of batter onto the griddle. Bake until bubbles start to form and burst, about 2 minutes. Flip and cook to set the other side, another 1 to 2 minutes. As the pancakes are ready, put them in a single layer on the baking sheet and keep warm in the oven until ready to serve.

5 // Stack the pancakes on plates, drizzle with the cheese mixture, and sprinkle with coarsely chopped nuts.

ORANGE RICOTTA PANCAKES

WITH CARAMELIZED FIG COMPOTE AND PISTACHIOS

SERVES 4; MAKES 12 TO 14 PANCAKES

Wonderfully moist, these subtly orange-flavored ricotta pancakes are also incredibly light and fluffy. The trick is to add the egg yolks and whites, which are first stiffly beaten, separately. An elegant compote of luscious fresh figs and a sprinkling of crunchy green pistachios are the crowning touches.

¾ cup all-purpose flour

½ teaspoon baking powder

2 tablespoons granulated sugar

Pinch of fine sea salt

1 cup fresh ricotta cheese (see Note)

¾ cup whole milk

3 large eggs, separated

½ teaspoon pure vanilla extract

Grated zest of 1 orange

Unsalted butter, for the griddle

Fig Compote (recipe opposite)

½ cup lightly toasted pistachios, coarsely chopped

Confectioners' sugar

Mint sprigs, optional

1 // Preheat the oven to 250°F. Line a baking sheet with parchment.

2 // Whisk together the flour, baking powder, granulated sugar, and salt in a large bowl. Combine the ricotta, milk, egg yolks, vanilla, and zest in a medium bowl and whisk until smooth.

3 // Beat the egg whites in an electric mixer until they hold stiff peaks.

4 // Add the ricotta mixture to the flour mixture, stirring gently until just combined. Whisk in a small amount of the egg whites to lighten the batter and then fold in the remaining whites using a rubber spatula.

5 // Heat a large cast-iron griddle or nonstick sauté pan over medium heat. Brush with butter and continue heating until the butter begins to foam. Drop scant ⅓ cupfuls of batter onto the griddle. Bake until bubbles start to form and burst, 3 to 4 minutes. Flip and cook to set the other side, about 2 minutes. As the pancakes are ready, put them in a single layer on the baking sheet and keep warm in the oven until ready to serve.

6 // Stack the pancakes on plates and top with the fig compote and a sprinkling of pistachios. Dust with confectioners' sugar and garnish with the mint sprigs, if desired.

FIG COMPOTE
SERVES 4

¾ pound fresh figs

4 tablespoons (½ stick) unsalted butter

¼ cup lightly packed dark brown sugar

¼ cup clover honey

Pinch of kosher salt

1 // Preheat the broiler. Cut the stem off of each fig and slice the figs into quarters.

2 // Put the butter, brown sugar, honey, and salt in a medium cast-iron or broiler-proof sauté pan. Cook for about 1 minute over high heat, stirring frequently, until the syrup begins to bubble. Add the figs and stir to coat them with the syrup.

3 // Put the pan under the broiler to caramelize the figs, swirling the pan a few times over the next 5 minutes to prevent the sugar and figs from burning. The figs are done when the syrup is thickened slightly and amber in color. Serve hot.

NOTE

If you can't find fresh ricotta, buy the kind you can find in the refrigerated section of the grocery store, put it in a fine-mesh strainer, and let it drain for 1 hour before using.

PINEAPPLE UPSIDE-DOWN PANCAKES

WITH PINEAPPLE-MAPLE BUTTER SAUCE

SERVES 4; MAKES ABOUT 14 PANCAKES

While pineapple upside-down cake—made with rings of canned pineapple and maraschino cherries—is a bit of a throwback, these pancakes are anything but!

7 tablespoons unsalted butter, plus more for the griddle

1½ cups all-purpose flour

5 tablespoons sugar

1 teaspoon baking powder

½ teaspoon baking soda

¼ teaspoon fine sea salt

1½ cups buttermilk

2 large eggs

½ teaspoon pure vanilla extract

¾ cup pure grade B maple syrup

2½ cups finely diced fresh pineapple

Fresh cherries

Mint sprigs, optional

1 // Melt 3 tablespoons of the butter. Cut the remaining 4 tablespoons into small pieces and put in the freezer.

2 // Whisk together the flour, 3 tablespoons of the sugar, the baking powder, baking soda, and salt in a medium bowl. Whisk together the buttermilk, eggs, vanilla, and melted butter in a small bowl. Add to the flour mixture and whisk until just combined. Cover and refrigerate for at least 30 minutes and up to 4 hours.

3 // Preheat the oven to 250°F. Line a baking sheet with parchment.

4 // Bring the maple syrup to a simmer in a small saucepan. Whisk in the cold butter, one piece at a time, until thickened. Remove from the heat and stir in ½ cup of the pineapple. Cover and keep warm.

5 // Heat a large cast-iron griddle or nonstick sauté pan over medium heat. Brush with butter and continue heating until the butter begins to foam. Drop scant ¼ cupfuls of batter onto the griddle. Bake until bubbles start to form and burst, about 2 minutes. Evenly sprinkle a few tablespoons of the remaining 2 cups chopped pineapple over the top and sprinkle the pineapple with a little of the remaining 2 tablespoons sugar. Carefully flip and cook to set and caramelize the other side, another 1 to 2 minutes. As the pancakes are ready, put them in a single layer on the baking sheet and keep warm in the oven until ready to serve.

6 // Stack the pancakes on plates, caramelized pineapple side up, and drizzle with the pineapple-maple butter sauce. Garnish with the fresh cherries and mint sprigs, if desired.

MINI GERMAN PANCAKES

WITH APPLE-CALVADOS CARAMEL SAUCE

SERVES 3 OR 4; MAKES 18 TO 24 PANCAKES
(depending on size of the tin)

Light, eggy, and almost popover-like, a German pancake (sometimes called a Dutch baby) is cooked in the oven, where it puffs like a soufflé and then falls. While the dish is usually made in a large cast-iron pan and served in wedges, it's just as easy and fun to bake them in muffin tins for a crowd. Apples are a traditional accompaniment, and this caramel sauce, heady with Calvados, is brimming with sweet apple goodness.

1 cup whole milk

6 large eggs

1 heaping tablespoon granulated sugar

1 teaspoon pure vanilla extract

1 teaspoon grated orange zest

1 cup all-purpose flour

¼ teaspoon fine sea salt

4 tablespoons (½ stick) unsalted butter, melted

Nonstick cooking spray

Apple-Calvados Caramel Sauce (recipe opposite)

¼ cup confectioners' sugar

1 heaping teaspoon ground cinnamon

Whipped Sour Cream (recipe opposite), optional

1 // Preheat the oven to 400°F.

2 // Combine the milk, eggs, granulated sugar, vanilla, and orange zest in a blender and blend until smooth. Add the flour and salt and blend until completely smooth, about 1 minute. Blend in the butter a little at a time in order to temper the eggs.

3 // Spray muffin tins well with nonstick cooking spray and pour ¼ cup of the batter into each tin, filling each about three-quarters full. Bake until puffy and golden on top, about 15 minutes. Transfer the muffin tins to a baking rack for a few minutes.

4 // Remove the individual pancakes to a platter. The pancakes will sink slightly in the center. Fill each pancake with some of the caramel sauce. Mix together the confectioners' sugar and cinnamon and dust the pancakes with the cinnamon-sugar. Serve with whipped cream, if desired.

APPLE-CALVADOS CARAMEL SAUCE

SERVES 3 OR 4

4 tablespoons (½ stick) unsalted butter

¾ cup packed light brown muscovado sugar

½ teaspoon ground cinnamon

1 Granny Smith apple, peeled, cored, and diced

1 Gala apple, peeled, cored, and diced

¼ cup Calvados or other apple brandy

¼ cup heavy cream

1 // Melt the butter in a large skillet over medium-high heat. Whisk in the sugar and cinnamon and cook until the sugar is melted and slightly thickened, 5 minutes. Add the apples and cook, stirring, until soft, about 8 minutes.

2 // Carefully add the Calvados and simmer until reduced and syrupy, 5 minutes. Pour in the cream and cook until warmed through, 2 minutes. Serve hot.

WHIPPED SOUR CREAM

MAKES ABOUT 1 CUP

¾ cup heavy cream

2 tablespoons sour cream

Combine the heavy cream and sour cream in the bowl of a stand mixer fitted with the whisk attachment and whip until soft peaks form. Cover and refrigerate for up to 1 hour before serving.

CHOCOLATE BLINTZES

WITH WHIPPED RICOTTA–ALMOND FILLING AND CHERRIES

SERVES 6 TO 8

Thin, unleavened blintzes are much like crepes. I like to fill cocoa-enriched blintzes with a smooth, fluffy mixture of chocolaty whipped ricotta and crunchy slivers of toasted almonds. A not-too-sweet sauce of dark cherries tops off this showstopping breakfast—or dessert. (Personally, I'm all for starting the day off on a chocolate high!)

Ricotta filling

2 cups fresh ricotta

3 tablespoons confectioners' sugar

2 tablespoons unsweetened cocoa powder

½ teaspoon pure vanilla extract

¼ cup toasted slivered almonds

1 ounce bittersweet chocolate, finely grated

Blintzes

2 large eggs

⅓ cup granulated sugar

2 cups whole milk

3 tablespoons unsalted butter, melted, plus more for the pan

1½ cups all-purpose flour

⅓ cup unsweetened cocoa powder

½ teaspoon fine sea salt

1 (12-ounce) jar Morello cherries in syrup

Confectioners' sugar

Mint sprigs, optional

continues

1 // Start the filling. Drain the ricotta in a fine-mesh sieve set over a bowl in the refrigerator for 4 hours.

2 // Whisk together the ricotta, confectioners' sugar, cocoa powder, and vanilla until light and fluffy. Fold in the almonds and chocolate, cover, and refrigerate for at least 1 hour and up to 8 hours.

3 // Make the blintz batter. Whisk together the eggs and granulated sugar until pale. Whisk in the milk and butter. Sift the flour, cocoa powder, and salt onto a piece of wax paper, add to the egg mixture, and whisk until smooth. Cover and refrigerate for at least 2 hours and up to 24 hours.

4 // Put the cherries and their syrup in a small saucepan and heat over low heat until warm, about 5 minutes.

5 // Cook the blintzes. Heat an 8- or 9-inch nonstick skillet over medium heat. Brush with butter and, when the butter sizzles, ladle a scant ¼ cup of batter into the skillet. Tilt the pan to swirl the batter so it covers the bottom of the skillet. Cook on one side until small air bubbles form and the top is set, a minute or two. Carefully loosen the edges of the blintz, flip over, and cook for 30 seconds on the second side. Slip out of the skillet onto a plate. Butter the skillet as needed and repeat until all the batter is used, stacking the blintzes on top of each other.

6 // Turn each blintz so the golden-brown side is up. Scoop 3 tablespoons of the filling in the middle of each in a 3-inch-long by 2-inch-wide mound. Roll once to cover the filling. Fold the sides into the center and continue rolling until completely closed. (You may have leftover filling, which I like to have on toast; do not be tempted to overfill the blintzes.)

7 // Serve 2 blintzes per plate. Spoon some of the warm cherries on top, sprinkle with the confectioners' sugar, and garnish with the mint sprigs, if desired.

PEANUT BUTTER FRENCH TOAST WAFFLES
WITH MIXED BERRY SAUCE

SERVES 4

Even as a grownup, I love how the flavors of pb&j go together—rich, nutty, ever-so-slightly salty peanut butter, and sweet fruit jam that's just a tiny bit tart. Awesome. These pb&j waffles start out as French toast before being cooked to dimpled, golden perfection in a waffle maker. A new brunch classic in the making.

8 (½-inch) slices good-quality white or whole-wheat bread, crusts removed

5 large eggs

1 cup whole or 2% milk

1 tablespoon granulated sugar

½ teaspoon pure vanilla extract

Pinch of fine sea salt

4 tablespoons smooth peanut butter

Nonstick cooking spray

Confectioners' sugar

Mixed Berry Sauce (page 51)

Mixed fresh berries

Mint sprigs, optional

1 // The night before, put the bread on a baking rack and let it sit out overnight until stale.

2 // The next day, crack the eggs into a medium baking dish and whisk lightly. Whisk in the milk, granulated sugar, vanilla, and salt.

3 // Spread 4 slices of the bread with 1 tablespoon of the peanut butter each. Top those slices with the remaining slices of bread to make 4 sandwiches. Press down on them to flatten slightly. Soak the bread in the egg mixture until completely soaked through, 2 to 3 minutes per side.

4 // Heat a square 4-slot waffle iron according to the manufacturer's directions. Spray the top and bottom grates liberally with nonstick spray.

5 // Remove the French toast from the baking dish using a slotted spatula, allowing excess egg mixture to drip off. Make 2 at a time. Press down gently at first, then add a little pressure to the cover, and press until the cover is completely closed. Cook until golden brown, about 3 minutes. Repeat with the remaining French toast sandwiches.

6 // Carefully remove each French toast waffle to a plate. Dust with confectioners' sugar and drizzle with some of the mixed berry sauce. Garnish with the fresh berries and mint sprigs, if desired.

COCONUT WAFFLES

WITH CHOCOLATE MAPLE SYRUP AND BANANA

SERVES 4

These waffles have amplified coconut flavor; there's toasted coconut both in and on top of the waffles and coconut milk in the batter. The result is a moist, sweet waffle with chewy shreds of coconut in each bite. Sliced bananas and a maple syrup doctored with chocolate are the perfect finish.

1¾ cups all-purpose flour

2 tablespoons granulated sugar

1 tablespoon light brown muscovado sugar

1 tablespoon baking powder

¼ teaspoon plus a pinch of fine sea salt

1¼ cups whole milk

3 large eggs

½ cup unsweetened coconut milk

½ teaspoon pure vanilla extract

6 tablespoons (¾ stick) unsalted butter, melted, plus more for the waffle iron

3 tablespoons canola oil

⅓ cup shredded sweetened coconut, lightly toasted, plus more for serving

1 cup pure grade B maple syrup

2 ounces bittersweet chocolate, finely chopped

2 large ripe bananas, sliced

1 // Preheat the oven to 250°F. Put a baking rack on top of a baking sheet.

2 // Whisk together the flour, both types of sugar, baking powder, and ¼ teaspoon of the salt in a medium bowl. Whisk together the milk, eggs, coconut milk, vanilla, butter, and oil in a medium bowl. Add to the flour mixture and mix until just combined. Gently fold in the coconut. Cover and let rest in the refrigerator for 30 minutes.

3 // Bring the maple syrup to a simmer in a small ovenproof saucepan over low heat, add the chocolate and remaining pinch of salt, and remove from the heat. Whisk until smooth. Keep warm in the oven until serving.

4 // Heat a waffle iron according to the manufacturer's directions. Brush the grates liberally with butter. Fill the iron and cook according to the manufacturer's instructions until crisp and golden. Transfer to the baking rack in the oven to keep warm while you cook more waffles, buttering the grates before each batch.

5 // Serve the waffles topped with the bananas, syrup, and a sprinkling of toasted coconut.

GINGERBREAD PUMPKIN WAFFLES

WITH BUTTERMILK-BOURBON CARAMEL SAUCE

SERVES 6; MAKES 12 WAFFLES

Richly spiced with cloves, nutmeg, cinnamon, and ginger, these wintry waffles get an additional boost of flavor from finely diced candied ginger. The rich, sweet sauce is the perfect complement; try this as dessert, too!

2 cups all-purpose flour

2 tablespoons granulated sugar

2 tablespoons light brown muscovado sugar

1 teaspoon baking powder

1 teaspoon baking soda

¼ teaspoon fine sea salt

1½ teaspoons ground cinnamon

1 teaspoon ground ginger

¼ teaspoon grated nutmeg

¼ teaspoon ground cloves

4 large eggs

1 cup whole milk

6 tablespoons (¾ stick) unsalted butter, melted, plus more for the waffle iron

½ cup sour cream

3 tablespoons molasses

½ cup canned pure pumpkin puree (not pie filling)

2 tablespoons finely diced candied ginger

Buttermilk-Bourbon Caramel Sauce (page 51)

1 // Preheat the oven to 250°F. Put a baking rack on top of a baking sheet.

2 // In a large bowl, whisk together the flour, both types of sugar, baking powder, baking soda, salt, cinnamon, ground ginger, nutmeg, and cloves. In a medium bowl, whisk together the eggs, milk, butter, sour cream, molasses, and pumpkin until smooth. Add to the flour mixture and whisk until just combined; fold in the candied ginger. Cover and let sit at room temperature for 15 minutes.

3 // Heat a waffle iron according to the manufacturer's directions. Brush the grates liberally with butter. Fill the iron and cook according to the manufacturer's instructions until crisp and golden. Transfer to the baking rack in the oven to keep warm while you cook more waffles, buttering the grates before each batch.

4 // Serve the waffles topped with the buttermilk-bourbon caramel sauce.

BELGIAN WAFFLES
WITH CINNAMON-SUGAR BUTTER
AND SAUTÉED CIDER APPLES

SERVES 8

Belgian waffles, crisp on the outside and tender inside, are distinguished by their deep pockets, which practically beg to be filled with pools of melted butter. So go ahead, use a heavy hand with the homemade cinnamon-sugar butter. Tart Granny Smith apples, sautéed in a sweetened, cinnamon-infused apple cider reduction, make this dish a fantastic choice for fall.

1¾ cups all-purpose flour

2 teaspoons baking powder

¼ teaspoon baking soda

½ teaspoon fine sea salt

3 tablespoons sugar

3 large eggs

8 tablespoons (1 stick) unsalted butter, melted, plus more for the waffle iron

1½ cups buttermilk

Homemade Cinnamon-Sugar Butter (page 60)

Sautéed Cider Apples (recipe opposite)

1 // Preheat the oven to 250°F. Put a baking rack on top of a baking sheet.

2 // Whisk together the flour, baking powder, baking soda, salt, and sugar in a medium bowl. Whisk together the eggs, butter, and buttermilk in a small bowl. Add to the flour mixture and mix until just combined. Do not overmix. Set the batter aside at room temperature for 20 minutes.

3 // Heat a waffle iron according to the manufacturer's directions. Brush the grates liberally with butter. Fill the iron and cook according to the manufacturer's instructions until crisp and golden. Transfer to the baking rack in the oven to keep warm while you cook more waffles, buttering the grates before each batch.

4 // Serve the waffles topped with some of the cinnamon-sugar butter and sautéed apples.

SAUTÉED CIDER APPLES
SERVES 8

  2 cups apple cider
  1 tablespoon light brown sugar
  2 cinnamon sticks
  2 tablespoons unsalted butter
  2 Granny Smith apples, peeled, cored, and thinly sliced

1 // Combine the cider, sugar, and cinnamon sticks in a large sauté pan over high heat and boil until reduced by half and thickened to a syrup, about 10 minutes.

2 // Remove the cinnamon sticks, whisk in the butter, and add the apples. Cook over medium heat until soft and caramelized, about 10 minutes. Serve hot.

CUBAN TORREJAS

WITH GUAVA MAPLE SYRUP

SERVES 4 TO 6

The French don't have a monopoly on custard-soaked, pan-fried bread. Cuban bread, much like traditional French or Italian white loaves, but made with lard or shortening, has a papery crust and soft interior that stales quickly, making it perfect for soaking up some eggy goodness. Keep the Cuban flavor going by serving your torrejas with a sweet guava maple syrup.

¾ cup pure grade B maple syrup

1 cinnamon stick

¼ cup guava marmalade

3 large egg yolks

1 cup whole milk

2 tablespoons sugar

½ teaspoon ground cinnamon, plus more for serving

1 teaspoon pure vanilla extract

3 large eggs, beaten

4 tablespoons canola oil

4 tablespoons (½ stick) unsalted butter

8 to 10 slices Cuban or French bread

Whipped cream

1 // Preheat the oven to 250°F. Line a baking sheet with parchment paper.

2 // Combine the syrup and cinnamon stick in a small ovenproof saucepan and bring to a simmer. Remove from the heat and let sit for 10 minutes. Remove the cinnamon stick, return to the heat, and bring to a simmer. Whisk in the marmalade. Keep warm in the oven while you make the torrejas.

3 // Whisk together the egg yolks, milk, sugar, ground cinnamon, and vanilla in a shallow bowl until smooth. In a separate shallow bowl, whisk the whole eggs until really frothy.

4 // Cook the toast in batches: Heat 2 tablespoons of the oil and 2 tablespoons of the butter in a large sauté pan over medium-high heat until the oil shimmers. Dip the bread into the yolk mixture, remove, and let the excess batter drip off; then dip in the whole egg mixture and let the excess drip off. Fry the bread in batches until golden brown, about 2 minutes on each side. Transfer to the baking sheet in the oven to keep warm while you cook the second batch.

5 // Serve the torrejas topped with the hot guava syrup, a dollop of whipped cream, and a sprinkling of cinnamon.

ALMOND CROISSANT FRENCH TOAST

WITH ALMOND BUTTER SYRUP

SERVES 4

I love a good almond croissant from a great French bakery—that is one thing I definitely leave to the professionals. But I do like to take regular croissants, which are pretty easy to find, and transform them into this decadent, buttery, nutty French toast, which has the same flavors. Be sure to use pure almond extract, as the flavor will really shine in the custard.

2 large eggs

2 large egg yolks

2 tablespoons granulated sugar

1¼ cups half-and-half

¼ teaspoon pure vanilla extract

¼ teaspoon pure almond extract

Pinch of fine sea salt

4 fresh all-butter croissants

½ cup Clarified Butter (recipe opposite)

Almond Butter Syrup (page 50)

Confectioners' sugar, optional

1 // Preheat the oven to 250°F. Line a baking sheet with parchment paper.

2 // Whisk together the eggs, yolks, and granulated sugar in a small baking dish until smooth. Whisk in the half-and-half, vanilla, almond extract, and salt.

3 // Cut the croissants almost in half lengthwise, leaving them attached on one long side, and open them up.

4 // Heat 2 tablespoons of the clarified butter in a medium sauté pan over medium heat until it begins to shimmer. Dip one of the croissants into the custard for 10 seconds, flip over, and soak the other side for 10 seconds. (Do not oversoak or it will fall apart because the croissant is fresh, not stale.) Carefully add it to the pan cut side down and cook until golden brown and a crust has formed, about 1½ minutes. Flip and cook until the bottom is crisp and golden brown too, another minute or so. Transfer to the baking sheet and repeat with the remaining croissants.

5 // Serve the croissants topped with the almond butter syrup and a dusting of confectioners' sugar, if desired.

CLARIFIED BUTTER
MAKES ¼ CUP

8 tablespoons (1 stick) unsalted butter

1 // Heat the butter in a small saucepan over very low heat until melted. Let simmer gently until the foam rises to the top of the melted butter. Remove from the heat and skim off the foam with a spoon. Discard the foam.

2 // Carefully pour the warm butter into a container, leaving behind any solids at the bottom of the pan. Let cool and then cover and refrigerate for up to 2 weeks.

BANANAS FOSTER FRENCH TOAST
WITH WHIPPED CREAM CHEESE

SERVES 4

Classic French toast, with its rich, custardy interior and crisp, buttery crust, is jazzed up with a topping inspired by New Orleans's own bananas Foster.

French toast

3 large eggs

4 large egg yolks

2 tablespoons granulated sugar

1 cup whole milk

½ cup heavy cream

1 teaspoon ground cinnamon

1 teaspoon pure vanilla extract

6 tablespoons (¾ stick) unsalted butter

6 tablespoons canola oil

8 (½-inch-thick) slices day-old brioche

Topping

4 tablespoons (½ stick) unsalted butter

1 cup packed light brown muscovado sugar

Pinch of ground cinnamon

2 small ripe bananas, cut into ½-inch-thick slices

½ cup dark rum

2 tablespoons banana liqueur

Whipped Cream Cheese (page 61)

Confectioners' sugar, optional

1 // Preheat the oven to 250°F. Line a baking sheet with parchment paper.

2 // Make the French toast. Whisk together the eggs, yolks, and granulated sugar until smooth. Whisk in the milk, cream, cinnamon, and vanilla.

3 // Cook the French toast in 3 batches. Heat 2 tablespoons of the butter and 2 tablespoons of the oil in a large sauté pan over medium heat until the butter is melted and the oil begins to shimmer. Put 3 slices of the bread in the custard mixture and let sit on both sides until soaked through, 30 seconds. Remove with a slotted spatula to allow the excess custard to run off, add to the pan, and cook until golden brown on both sides and cooked through, about 2 minutes per side. Transfer to the baking sheet in the oven. Repeat with the remaining ingredients.

4 // Make the topping. Heat the butter in a large sauté pan over high heat until it begins to sizzle. Whisk in the brown sugar and cinnamon and cook until the sugar has melted and the mixture has thickened slightly, 5 minutes.

5 // Add the bananas and cook until slightly softened, 1 minute. Remove from the heat, add the rum and banana liqueur, return to the heat, and cook until the alcohol has burned off, 2 minutes.

6 // Serve 2 slices of French toast per person, topped with some of the bananas and syrup, a dollop of whipped cream cheese, and a sprinkling of confectioners' sugar, if desired.

BRÛLÉED ORANGE FRENCH TOAST

WITH ORANGE SYRUP

SERVES 4

If you're really looking for a brunch dish to impress, stop here. Nothing brings out the oohs and aahs like a kitchen torch, and what that torch does to this dish is magic. Rich, custardy, orange-scented French toast gets a bonus layer of delicious texture thanks to a crisp topping of caramelized sugar. The orange syrup, glossy with butter and punctuated with bright segments of orange, has just the right touch of bitterness to balance the sweetness.

3 large eggs

4 large egg yolks

1 cup whole milk

½ cup heavy cream

1 teaspoon grated orange zest

¼ cup fresh orange juice

2 tablespoons firmly packed light brown sugar

2 tablespoons plus 8 teaspoons granulated sugar

2 teaspoons pure vanilla extract

1 tablespoon orange liqueur, such as Grand Marnier

½ teaspoon fine sea salt

8 (1¾-inch-thick) day-old slices brioche

6 tablespoons (¾ stick) unsalted butter, plus more
    for serving

3 tablespoons canola oil

Orange Syrup (page 54)

1 // In a baking dish, whisk together the eggs, yolks, milk, cream, orange zest, orange juice, brown sugar, 2 tablespoons of the granulated sugar, vanilla, orange liqueur, and salt until combined. Soak the bread slices in the egg mixture until completely soaked through, at least 15 to 30 seconds per side.

2 // Cook the French toast in batches (3 slices at a time) in a large sauté pan. Heat 2 tablespoons of the butter and 1 tablespoon of the oil in the pan over medium-high heat until it begins to sizzle. Add the bread and cook, turning once, until golden and crisp, about 2 minutes per side.

3 // Transfer the French toast to a baking sheet. Sprinkle the remaining 8 teaspoons granulated sugar evenly over the surface of the French toast, using 1 teaspoon per piece. Using a kitchen torch according to the manufacturer's instructions, move the flame continuously in small circles over the surface until the sugar melts and lightly browns.

4 // Serve 2 slices of toast per person, spooning the orange syrup on top.

PAIN PERDU

WITH FRESH PEACHES
AND VANILLA BEAN BUTTER

SERVES 4

Extra thick, with a custardy interior and crunchy exterior, this recipe makes all other "French" toast green with envy.

2 ripe peaches, skinned, pitted, and sliced into eighths

2 ripe white peaches, skinned, pitted, and sliced into eighths

¼ cup plus 2 tablespoons granulated sugar

2 tablespoons light brown muscovado sugar

2 tablespoons peach eau de vie

4 large eggs

2 large egg yolks

¼ teaspoon fine sea salt

1 teaspoon ground cinnamon

¼ teaspoon grated nutmeg

2 cups whole milk, plus more if needed

½ cup heavy cream

2 teaspoons pure vanilla extract

8 (¾-inch-thick) slices day-old brioche

6 tablespoons (¾ stick) unsalted butter

6 tablespoons canola oil

4 cups French feuilletine or cornflakes, crushed

Vanilla Bean Butter (page 60)

1 // Preheat the oven to 350°F. Line a baking sheet with parchment.

2 // Combine the peaches, 2 tablespoons of the granulated sugar, the muscovado sugar, and the peach eau de vie in a large bowl and let macerate at room temperature for 30 minutes.

3 // Strain the peach juices into a large sauté pan and boil over high heat until reduced and caramelized, about 5 minutes. Add the peaches and heat through, about 5 minutes. Keep warm.

4 // Whisk together the whole eggs, yolks, and remaining ¼ cup sugar in a baking dish until combined. Add the salt, cinnamon, nutmeg, milk, cream, and vanilla and whisk until smooth. Add the bread, in batches, and soak on each side for 30 seconds.

5 // While the bread is soaking, cook the French toast in 3 batches. Heat 2 tablespoons of the butter and 2 tablespoons of the oil in a large sauté pan over medium-high heat until the butter is melted and the oil begins to shimmer.

6 // Spread the feuilletine in a baking dish and dip the bread on each side into the mixture, pressing to adhere. Cook 3 slices of the bread on each side until golden brown. Transfer to the baking sheet. Repeat with the remaining ingredients.

7 // Bake in the oven just to heat through completely, about 5 minutes.

8 // Serve 2 pieces per person, topping each with a dollop of the vanilla butter and spoonfuls of the caramelized peaches.

EGG
DISHES

STEAK AU POIVRE RATATOUILLE HASH

SERVES 4 TO 6

This one is straight from the brasserie: beefy hanger steak, pepper crusted and cooked to perfection. Cubes of creamy Yukon gold potatoes are folded into a ratatouille-like sauté of the Provençal favorites, bell peppers, tomatoes, zucchini, and garlic. A healthy dose of verdant chopped parsley finishes the dish.

2 large Yukon gold potatoes

Kosher salt and freshly ground black pepper

7 tablespoons canola oil

12 ounces hanger steak

1 medium red onion, diced

1 medium red bell pepper, diced

1 medium yellow bell pepper, diced

1 zucchini, diced

3 garlic cloves, finely chopped

1 cup grape tomatoes

2 teaspoons chopped fresh thyme

½ cup chopped fresh flat-leaf parsley

4 to 6 poached eggs (see page 107)

1 // Put the potatoes in a saucepan, add enough cold water to cover by 2 inches, season with salt, and bring to a boil over high heat. Lower the heat to medium and cook the potatoes until they are not quite tender when pierced with a knife, 25 minutes. Drain, let cool, and then dice.

2 // Heat 2 tablespoons of the oil in a large sauté pan over high heat until it begins to shimmer. Season the steak on both sides with salt and crust one side of the steak with 2 teaspoons coarsely ground black pepper. Put the steak in the pan, pepper side down, and cook until golden brown, 3 to 4 minutes. Flip over and continue cooking to medium-rare, 4 to 5 minutes longer. Remove to a plate, tent loosely with foil, and let rest for 10 minutes before cutting into dice.

3 // Heat 2 tablespoons of the oil in a large cast-iron skillet over high heat. Add the potatoes, season with salt and pepper, and cook until lightly golden brown on all sides. Remove to a plate.

4 // Heat the remaining 3 tablespoons oil in the pan, add the onion, bell peppers, and zucchini and cook, stirring a few times, until soft, about 5 minutes. Add the garlic and tomatoes and cook for 1 minute. Return the potatoes to the pan, add the steak, thyme, and parsley, and cook until the mixture is heated through, about 5 minutes longer; season with salt and pepper.

5 // Transfer the hash to a platter and top with the poached eggs.

TARTE FLAMBÉ
WITH SOFTLY SCRAMBLED EGGS AND GOAT CHEESE

SERVES 6

Alsatian Tarte flambé is a thin-crust pizza layered with caramelized onion and smoky bacon. I up the ante with herbs, scrambled eggs, and creamy goat cheese.

½ cup crème fraîche

2 tablespoons fresh flat-leaf parsley leaves, plus more for serving

2 tablespoons chopped fresh chives, plus more for serving

1 tablespoon fresh tarragon leaves, plus more for serving

Kosher salt and freshly ground black pepper

1 pound store-bought pizza dough

2 tablespoons canola oil, plus more for brushing

4 tablespoons (½ stick) unsalted butter

1 large Vidalia onion, halved and thinly sliced

Pinch of sugar

½ pound double-smoked bacon, cut crosswise into lardons (short, thick matchsticks)

2 cups grated sharp white cheddar

1 Fresno chile, finely diced

6 large eggs

2 ounces soft goat cheese, cut into small pieces and frozen for 5 minutes

1 // Whisk together the crème fraîche, parsley, chives, and tarragon in a bowl; season with salt and pepper. Cover and refrigerate for 30 minutes.

2 // Preheat the oven to 400°F.

3 // Divide the dough in half. Roll each piece into a very thin 12 × 10-inch rectangle. Brush with oil, place on baking sheets, and bake until lightly golden brown, about 10 minutes.

4 // Heat 1 tablespoon of the oil and 1 tablespoon of the butter in a small sauté pan over medium heat. Add the onion and sugar and cook slowly, stirring occasionally, until caramelized, 30 minutes. Season with salt and pepper.

5 // Heat the remaining 1 tablespoon oil in a medium sauté pan over medium heat. Add the bacon and cook until golden brown and crisp, about 10 minutes. Remove with a slotted spoon to a plate lined with paper towels.

6 // Divide the crème fraîche between the pizzas, spreading it out. Divide the cheddar on top and then add the onion and bacon. Bake until the cheese has melted, about 5 minutes.

7 // Meanwhile, heat the remaining 3 tablespoons butter in a medium nonstick sauté pan over medium heat. Add the chile and cook until soft, about 2 minutes. Whisk the eggs in a bowl until smooth; season with salt and pepper. Pour the eggs into the pan and stir constantly with a rubber spatula until soft curds form. Add the goat cheese.

8 // Divide the eggs between the two pizzas and garnish with more herbs.

MOLE-RUBBED STEAK AND EGGS
WITH CHOCOLATE STOUT BEURRE BLANC

SERVES 4

I'm a lover of mole, the rich, chocolate-based, savory sauce from Oaxaca, Mexico, but it is admittedly time-consuming to make. This rub—a blend of earthy, savory spices, cocoa powder, and brown sugar—is an excellent way to get that full mole flavor without the wait. Chocolate stout lends a dark complexity to the rich sauce, and the taste echoes that of the mole rub.

Steak

3 tablespoons ancho chile powder

1 tablespoon New Mexican chile powder

½ teaspoon chile de árbol powder

2 teaspoons unsweetened cocoa powder

2 teaspoons light brown sugar

1 teaspoon ground cinnamon

¼ teaspoon ground allspice

¼ teaspoon ground cloves

¼ teaspoon coarsely ground black pepper

1½ pounds New York strip steak (1½ inches thick)

2 tablespoons canola oil, plus more for brushing

Kosher salt

Sauce

1 large shallot, finely diced

1 cup chocolate stout

2 cups beef or chicken stock, preferably homemade

4 tablespoons (½ stick) unsalted butter, cut into small pieces, cold

1 tablespoon finely chopped fresh flat-leaf parsley, plus more for serving

1 teaspoon finely chopped fresh thyme

Kosher salt and freshly ground black pepper

4 large eggs

1 // Season the steak. Stir together the three chile powders, cocoa powder, sugar, cinnamon, allspice, cloves, and pepper in a small bowl. Brush the steak on both sides with oil and season with salt. Rub one side of the steak with the rub and let sit at room temperature for 30 minutes.

2 // Heat the oil in a large sauté pan over high heat. Add the steak, rub side down, and cook until golden brown and a crust has formed, about 4 minutes. Turn the steak over, reduce the heat to medium, and continue cooking until the bottom is golden brown and cooked to medium-rare, 5 to 6 minutes longer. Remove from the heat, cover, and let rest for 10 minutes while you make the pan sauce.

3 // Make the sauce. Return the pan to medium heat, add the shallot and cook until soft, a few minutes. Add the stout and simmer until almost completely reduced, about 5 minutes. Add the stock and simmer until reduced to 1 cup, about 5 minutes. Remove the pan from the heat and whisk in the cold butter piece by piece until emulsified. Add the parsley and thyme and season with salt and pepper. Keep warm.

4 // Cook the eggs as desired, whether poached (see Note), scrambled, or sunny side up.

5 // Slice the meat on the bias into ¼-inch-thick slices. Serve topped with the eggs and drizzled with some of the sauce. Garnish with parsley.

NOTE

To poach eggs, heat 3 cups water with 1 tablespoon white vinegar until simmering in a large high-sided frying pan. Break each egg into a cup and then gently add to the water. Poach until the yolks are nearly set, 4 to 5 minutes. Remove the eggs from the pan with a slotted spoon to drain the liquid and place on a plate. Season with salt and pepper.

FRITTATA

WITH PEPPERS, ONIONS, AND ROASTED CHERRY TOMATO SAUCE

SERVES 4 TO 6

This Italian frittata, laced with sweet ribbons of peppers and onions and seasoned with oregano and nutty Parmesan cheese, is a great make-ahead dish. Serve it topped with a quick sauce of oven-roasted cherry tomatoes, garlic, and basil.

2 tablespoons olive oil

1 red bell pepper, seeded and thinly sliced

1 yellow bell pepper, seeded and thinly sliced

1 medium Spanish onion, halved and thinly sliced

Kosher salt and freshly ground black pepper

8 large eggs

⅓ cup freshly grated Parmigiano-Reggiano

1 tablespoon finely chopped fresh oregano

¼ cup chopped fresh flat-leaf parsley

Roasted Cherry Tomato Sauce (recipe follows)

1 // Preheat the broiler.

2 // Heat the oil in a 12-inch ovenproof nonstick skillet over medium-high heat. Add the bell peppers and onion, season with salt and pepper, and cook, stirring occasionally, until softened, 5 minutes.

3 // Whisk together the eggs, Parmigiano-Reggiano, and oregano until light and fluffy; season with salt and pepper. Pour the egg mixture into the pan and stir with a heatproof silicone spatula. Cook until the egg mixture has set on the bottom and begins to set on top, 4 to 5 minutes. Put the pan underneath the broiler and cook until lightly browned and fluffy, 3 to 4 minutes.

4 // Carefully slide the frittata onto a cutting board. Sprinkle with parsley, cut into wedges, and top with some of the sauce. Serve hot or at room temperature.

ROASTED CHERRY TOMATO SAUCE

SERVES 4 TO 6

1 pint cherry tomatoes

2 garlic cloves, thinly sliced

3 tablespoons olive oil

Kosher salt and freshly ground black pepper

¼ cup chopped fresh basil

1 // Preheat the oven to 375°F.

2 // Toss the tomatoes and garlic with the oil on a baking sheet and season with salt and pepper. Roast in the oven, stirring occasionally, until the cherry tomatoes are soft and their flavor has concentrated, about 30 minutes.

3 // Remove to a bowl and stir in the basil. Serve warm or at room temperature.

CRAB CAKES BENEDICT

WITH "OLD BAY" HOLLANDAISE
ON JOHNNYCAKES

SERVES 4 OR 8

This decadent take on eggs Benedict might as well have a Maryland state flag sticking out of it. I serve this multilayered dish at my restaurant Bar Americain as "The Preakness Benedict," in honor of Maryland's contribution to horse racing's Triple Crown, and I think it would be just the thing to fuel a day at the races!

½ cup mayonnaise

2 tablespoons Dijon mustard

2 heaping tablespoons prepared horseradish, drained

1 tablespoon fresh lemon juice

¼ teaspoon chile de árbol or cayenne pepper

Kosher salt and freshly ground black pepper

1½ pounds jumbo lump crabmeat, picked over

2 green onions, green and pale green parts, thinly sliced, plus more for serving

2 to 3 tablespoons Wondra flour

2½ cups panko

¼ cup canola oil

Johnny Griddle Cakes (page 239)

8 poached eggs (see page 107)

"Old Bay" Hollandaise (page 112)

1 // Whisk together the mayonnaise, mustard, horseradish, lemon juice, and chile de árbol in a bowl and season with salt and pepper. Add the crab and green onions and gently fold with a spatula to combine. Add enough of the Wondra flour just to bind the mixture. Cover and refrigerate for at least 1 hour and up to 8 hours.

2 // Preheat the oven to 300°F.

3 // Spread the panko onto a large platter or baking sheet and season with salt and pepper. Remove the crab mixture from the refrigerator and divide into 8 equal patties, each about ½ inch thick. Dredge the cakes on both sides in the panko and place on a platter.

4 // Heat the oil in a large ovenproof nonstick sauté pan over high heat until the oil begins to ripple. Sauté the cakes until golden brown on both sides, about 3 minutes per side. Transfer to the oven to heat through, about 10 minutes.

5 // Put a johnnycake on each plate, top each with a crab cake and then an egg, and spoon hollandaise sauce over the top. Garnish with sliced green onion.

"OLD BAY" HOLLANDAISE

SERVES 4

3 large egg yolks, lightly beaten

1 tablespoon fresh lemon juice

12 tablespoons (1½ sticks) unsalted butter, melted until foamy

2 teaspoons "Old Bay" Seasoning, store-bought or home-made (recipe opposite)

1 teaspoon kosher salt

¼ teaspoon freshly ground black pepper

Bring 2 inches of water to a simmer in a saucepan. Whisk together the egg yolks and lemon juice in a medium stainless-steel bowl and set over the simmering water. Whisk the yolks until pale yellow and fluffy, about 3 minutes. Slowly add the melted butter, a few tablespoons at a time, and whisk until thickened. Season the sauce with the spice mixture, salt, and pepper. Serve warm; you can keep the sauce in a double boiler for up to 15 minutes until ready to use.

"OLD BAY" SEASONING

MAKES ABOUT ¼ CUP

1 tablespoon ground bay leaves (I use a coffee grinder)

2½ teaspoons celery salt

1½ teaspoons dry mustard

1 teaspoon sweet Spanish paprika

1 teaspoon freshly ground black pepper

½ teaspoon ground white pepper

½ teaspoon freshly grated nutmeg

½ teaspoon ground cloves

¼ teaspoon ground allspice

¼ teaspoon ground ginger

¼ teaspoon red pepper flakes

¼ teaspoon ground cardamom

Stir together the spices in a small bowl. Store in a container with a tight-fitting lid in a cool, dark place for up to 1 month.

SAUTÉED BITTER GREEN OMELET

SERVES 2

Not all southern food is butter soaked or deep fried; this healthy omelet stuffed with baby greens is a great example. Appealingly bitter and tangy, thanks to a small dose of vinegar and hot sauce, the greens are sautéed in bacon fat for a smoky, savory note before being encased in a fluffy omelet.

3 tablespoons unsalted butter, cut into tablespoons

4 ounces pancetta or double-smoked bacon, cut into small dice

1 small red onion, halved and thinly sliced

2 garlic cloves, thinly sliced

1 pound bitter baby greens, such as mustard greens, dandelion, or beet greens

¼ cup vegetable or chicken stock or water

Kosher salt and freshly ground black pepper

Few dashes of chipotle hot sauce

Splash of white wine vinegar

6 large eggs

Chopped fresh flat-leaf parsley

1 // Melt 1 tablespoon of the butter in a 10-inch nonstick pan over medium heat. Add the pancetta and cook until golden brown and crisp and the fat has rendered, about 10 minutes. Remove with a slotted spoon to a plate lined with paper towels.

2 // Increase the heat under the pan to high, add the onion, and cook, stirring occasionally, until very soft, about 5 minutes. Add the garlic and cook for 1 minute. Add the greens and stock and cook until the greens are just wilted, about 5 minutes. Season with salt and pepper, stir in the hot sauce, vinegar, and cooked pancetta, and remove the greens to a bowl. Wipe out the pan with a paper towel.

3 // Return the pan to medium heat. Add the remaining 2 tablespoons butter and cook until the butter begins to shimmer. Whisk the eggs in a bowl until light and fluffy and season with salt and pepper. Pour the eggs into the pan and let the eggs cook until the bottom starts to set, about 1 minute. With a heat-resistant silicone spatula, gently push one edge of the egg up into the center of the pan, while tilting the pan to allow the still liquid egg to flow underneath. Repeat with the other edges, until there's no liquid left. Put the greens down the center of the omelet and roll into a cylinder.

4 // Flip the omelet onto a platter, season the top with salt and pepper, and sprinkle with chopped parsley.

SPANISH TORTILLA

WITH CHORIZO, PIQUILLO PEPPERS, AND ROASTED JALAPEÑO PESTO

SERVES 6 TO 8

The only thing the Spanish tortilla, a thick, open-faced potato omelet, has in common with its Mexican counterpart is its shape. This tortilla is a meal—be it breakfast, lunch, or dinner. Richly spiced, porky chorizo and piquillo peppers, which are at once spicy, sweet, and a touch smoky, both add tons of flavor to the tortilla, and Garrotxa, a piquant aged Spanish goat cheese, melts into every tangy, flavorful bite. I love how this dish covers so many bases—no need for a side of hash browns or sausage here. The potatoes and chorizo are already baked right in!

4 (2- to 2½-inch) small new potatoes

Kosher salt and freshly ground black pepper

3 tablespoons canola oil

½ pound fresh chorizo, preferably homemade (page 247)

1 dozen large eggs

¼ cup heavy cream

6 jarred piquillo peppers, cut into small dice

4 ounces Garrotxa cheese or Monterey Jack, grated (about 1 cup)

¼ cup chopped fresh flat-leaf parsley leaves

Roasted Jalapeño Pesto (page 116)

1 // Put the potatoes in a small saucepan, add enough cold water to cover by 1 inch, season with salt, and bring to a boil over medium heat. Cook until the potatoes are tender when pierced with a knife, 15 minutes. Drain, cool, and then slice ¼ inch thick.

2 // Heat 2 tablespoons of the oil in a large nonstick sauté pan over high heat. Add the chorizo and cook until golden brown, about 5 minutes. Remove with a slotted spoon to a plate lined with paper towels. Add the remaining 1 tablespoon oil to the pan and heat until it begins to shimmer. Add the potatoes and cook until lightly golden brown, 5 minutes.

3 // Whisk together the eggs and cream in a large bowl until pale and fluffy. Add the peppers, cheese, parsley, and chorizo and season with salt and pepper. Add the egg mixture to the pan with the potatoes, moving it around in the pan to get underneath the potatoes. Cook, stirring occasionally, until the bottom is lightly golden brown and set, 5 minutes.

4 // Place a large plate over the pan and carefully flip the tortilla onto it. Slide the tortilla back into the pan to cook the other side until golden brown, about 3 minutes.

5 // Slide the tortilla onto a cutting board, cut into wedges, and serve warm or at room temperature, with the pesto.

ROASTED JALAPEÑO PESTO
MAKES ¾ CUP

8 jalapeños

Canola oil

Kosher salt and freshly ground black pepper

1¼ cups tightly packed fresh cilantro leaves

1 garlic clove, chopped

3 tablespoons pine nuts

½ cup extra-virgin olive oil, or more if needed

¼ cup freshly grated Parmigiano-Reggiano

Splash of red wine vinegar

1 // Preheat the oven to 400°F.

2 // Toss the jalapeños in a few tablespoons canola oil and season with salt and pepper. Roast in an even layer on a baking sheet until soft and the skin is blistered, about 15 minutes. Remove the jalapeños to a bowl, cover with plastic wrap, and let sit for 15 minutes. Remove the stems and seeds; do not remove the blistered skin for this particular recipe.

3 // Combine the jalapeños, cilantro, garlic, and pine nuts in a food processor and process until coarsely chopped. With the motor running, slowly add the oil through the feed tube and process until smooth. Add the cheese, season with salt and pepper, and pulse a few times just to combine. If the mixture is too thick, add a few more teaspoons of oil and pulse. Transfer to a bowl and stir in the vinegar. The pesto will keep, covered in the refrigerator, for up to 24 hours. Serve at room temperature.

FRITTATA DI PANE

WITH BROCCOLI RABE, SAUSAGE, AND RICOTTA

SERVES 6

Pleasantly bitter broccoli rabe, fennel-seeded Italian sausage, and creamy ricotta work just as well in this savory bread pudding as they do tossed with pasta.

1 dozen large eggs

¼ cup heavy cream

¼ cup whole milk

½ cup grated Parmigiano-Reggiano, plus more for serving

Kosher salt and freshly ground black pepper

Scant 2 cups ½-inch-cubed day-old Italian bread, crusts removed

1 bunch broccoli rabe

2 tablespoons olive oil

3 hot or sweet pork or turkey sausage links, meat removed from casings (about ½ pound)

1 small onion, halved and thinly sliced

3 garlic cloves, finely chopped

Pinch of red pepper flakes

2 tablespoons unsalted butter

1 cup part-skim ricotta

¼ cup finely chopped fresh flat-leaf parsley

1 // Preheat the oven to 350°F.

2 // In a large bowl, whisk together the eggs, cream, milk, cheese, and salt and pepper to taste. Add the bread cubes and soak for 15 minutes.

3 // Bring a large saucepan of salted water to a boil. Have ready a medium bowl filled with ice water. Add the broccoli rabe to the boiling water and cook until just tender, about 2 minutes. Drain and transfer to the ice water to cool. Drain well.

4 // Heat the oil in a 10- or 12-inch ovenproof skillet over high heat until it begins to shimmer. Add the sausage and cook, breaking it up into small pieces with a wooden spoon, until golden brown, about 7 minutes. Remove the sausage to a plate lined with paper towels.

5 // Add the onion to the pan and cook until soft, about 4 minutes. Add the garlic and red pepper flakes and cook for 30 seconds. Add the broccoli rabe and toss to coat. Return the sausage to the pan and cook for a few minutes for the flavors to meld. Add the butter and reduce the heat to medium.

6 // Gently fold the bread pudding mixture into the pan and even the top. Add the ricotta by tablespoonfuls on top. Continue cooking, without stirring, until the bottom of the frittata is lightly browned, about 5 minutes.

7 // Transfer the skillet to the oven and cook until the center is firm to the touch, 15 to 20 minutes. Remove from the oven and sprinkle with the parsley. Let rest for 10 minutes. Cut into wedges and serve hot or at room temperature with additional grated cheese.

HANG TOWN FRY

SERVES 2

An omelet of bacon and oysters, hang town fry is a California Gold Rush original, first made for a prospector who had struck it rich and demanded the most expensive dish he could get. I like to honor the classic with smooth and tangy crème fraîche, crisp fried oysters, and thick-cut lardons of salty bacon.

¼ cup plus 2 teaspoons canola oil

2 ounces thick-cut slab bacon, cut into lardons (short, thick matchsticks)

1 teaspoon sugar

½ cup all-purpose flour

Kosher salt and freshly ground black pepper

8 West Coast oysters, shucked

4 large eggs

2 tablespoons crème fraîche

1 tablespoon unsalted butter

Arugula with Tomato Vinaigrette (page 216)

Thinly sliced green onion

1 // Heat 2 teaspoons of the oil in an 8-inch nonstick sauté pan over medium heat. Add the bacon and sugar and slowly cook until the fat has rendered and the bacon is crisp, about 8 minutes. Remove to a plate lined with paper towels.

2 // Add the remaining ¼ cup oil to the pan and heat over medium-high heat until the oil begins to shimmer. Meanwhile, put the flour on a plate and season with salt and pepper. Season the oysters with salt and pepper, dredge in the flour, and shake off the excess. Fry the oysters until golden brown on both sides and just cooked through, 3 minutes total. Remove the oysters to a plate lined with paper towels, carefully discard the oil in the pan, and wipe the pan clean with a paper towel.

3 // Whisk together the eggs and crème fraîche and season with salt and pepper. Return the pan to the stove over medium heat. Add the butter and heat until it begins to sizzle. Add the oysters and eggs and cook, stirring constantly, until soft curds form, about 2 minutes.

4 // Divide between 2 plates and top with the dressed arugula. Drizzle with more of the vinaigrette and garnish with the crisp bacon and sliced green onion.

OLIVE OIL–POACHED EGGS
WITH CRISP PANCETTA AND
TOMATO–MUSTARD SEED RELISH

SERVES 4

I absolutely love this dish. Layered on sourdough toast with crisp slices of pancetta and a barely cooked tomato relish popping with the bright flavor of toasted mustard seeds, these silky poached eggs are a must-try for brunch.

Canola oil

8 thin slices pancetta

Kosher salt and freshly ground black pepper

1 cup extra-virgin olive oil

1 garlic clove

4 large eggs

4 slices sourdough bread, lightly toasted

Tomato–Mustard Seed Relish (recipe follows)

Chopped fresh flat-leaf parsley, for garnish

Chopped chives, for garnish

1 // Preheat the oven to 375°F.

2 // Brush a baking sheet lightly with canola oil and add the pancetta in an even layer, leaving a little room between slices. Sprinkle the top with black pepper. Bake until just crisp, about 8 minutes. Set aside to cool.

3 // Put the olive oil and garlic in a small sauté pan over medium heat. Heat until the garlic begins to sizzle and turns light golden brown, about 1 minute. Remove the garlic and discard. Bring the oil to 140°F on an instant-read thermometer.

4 // Crack each egg into a ramekin and carefully slide the eggs, one at a time, into the warm oil. Poach until the yolks are almost set, about 3 minutes.

5 // Put each piece of toast on a plate. Remove the eggs with a slotted spoon and place one on top of each piece of toast; season with salt and pepper. Top each egg with 2 pieces of pancetta and some of the tomato relish. Garnish with parsley and chives.

TOMATO–MUSTARD SEED RELISH
SERVES 4

3 tablespoons olive oil

1 teaspoon yellow mustard seeds

½ pint heirloom cherry tomatoes, quartered

Pinch of sugar

Kosher salt and freshly ground black pepper

Splash of red wine vinegar

2 tablespoons chopped fresh flat-leaf parsley

2 tablespoons chopped fresh chives

Heat the oil in a large sauté pan over medium heat, add the mustard seeds, and cook until the seeds begin to pop, about 30 seconds. Add the tomatoes, sugar, and salt and pepper to taste and cook until the tomatoes begin to just soften, about 5 minutes. Add the vinegar, parsley, and chives and transfer to a bowl. Serve warm or at room temperature.

POACHED EGGS IN MOLE
WITH CREAMY GREEN RICE

SERVES 4

There's no getting around it: mole is a time-consuming, ingredient-heavy endeavor. Equally inescapable: just how rich, complex, and flat-out delicious the savory, chocolate-laced Mexican sauce can be. Oven poaching the eggs in the mole itself is traditional and yields incredibly flavorful eggs. The creamy green rice, rich with heavy cream and colored by peppery roasted poblanos, bright cilantro, and pungent green onions, is a Mesa Grill classic.

Mole

¼ cup slivered raw almonds

2 tablespoons canola oil

1 small Spanish onion, coarsely chopped

3 garlic cloves, coarsely chopped

1 cup pureed plum tomatoes

3 cups chicken stock

Scant ¼ cup pureed canned chipotle in adobo

2 tablespoons ancho chile powder

1 tablespoon New Mexican chile powder

½ teaspoon ground chile de árbol

¼ cup chopped fresh mango

¼ cup golden raisins

¼ cup crushed blue corn tortilla chips

3 tablespoons molasses

1 tablespoon honey

1 tablespoon pure grade B maple syrup

1 teaspoon ground cinnamon

½ teaspoon ground cloves

½ teaspoon ground allspice

1 ounce semisweet or bittersweet chocolate, finely chopped

Kosher salt and freshly ground black pepper

4 large eggs

Kosher salt and freshly ground black pepper

Green Rice (page 240), hot

¼ pound queso fresco, crumbled

¼ pound grated cotija cheese

Fresh cilantro leaves

1 // Make the mole. Put the almonds in a medium saucepan over medium heat and cook, stirring occasionally, until lightly golden brown, about 5 minutes. Remove the almonds to a plate. Increase the heat under the pan to high, add the oil, and heat until it begins to shimmer. Add the onion and cook until soft, about 4 minutes. Add the garlic and cook for 30 seconds. Stir in the tomatoes, chicken stock, chipotle, and three chile powders, bring to a boil, and boil for 10 minutes.

2 // Add the mango, raisins, tortilla chips, and almonds, lower the heat, and cook, stirring occasionally, until the mango is soft and the mixture is reduced by half, about 30 minutes.

3 // Carefully transfer the mixture to a blender and blend until smooth. Return the mixture to the pan over high heat, add the molasses, honey, maple syrup, cinnamon, cloves, allspice, and chocolate, and boil until reduced to a sauce consistency, about 10 minutes. Season with salt and pepper.

4 // Preheat the oven to 350°F.

5 // Pour the mole into a medium high-sided ovenproof sauté pan and bring to a simmer over medium heat. Crack the eggs, one a time, into a ramekin and carefully transfer to the mole. Season the tops of the eggs with salt and pepper. Transfer the pan to the oven and cook until the whites are just set and the yolks are still jiggly, about 5 minutes.

6 // Spoon the rice into shallow bowls and make an indention in the center of each serving. Put an egg in the center and spoon some of the mole over the egg. Sprinkle with the cheeses and garnish with the cilantro leaves.

CHILE OIL

MAKES ABOUT 1¼ CUPS

¼ cup stemmed and finely chopped fresh
   Tutto Calabria hot long chile peppers
   or hot cherry peppers

1 cup extra-virgin olive oil

¼ teaspoon kosher salt

Combine the chopped chiles, oil, and salt in
a small saucepan over low heat and cook for
5 minutes. Remove from the heat and let cool
completely. Transfer to a bowl, cover, and
refrigerate for up to 1 week.

CREAMY POLENTA

WITH BRAISED GREENS, POACHED EGGS, AND CHILE OIL

SERVES 4

This rustic Italian dish feeds body and soul. Creamy polenta is comforting and filling and perfectly complemented by earthy, vinegary braised mustard greens and a poached egg. I like to top everything off with a touch of heat; chile oil, made with the well-balanced spicy, fruity, smoky, salty Calabrian long chile pepper, does just the trick.

Polenta

1 cup whole milk

1 teaspoon kosher salt

¼ teaspoon freshly ground black pepper

1 cup polenta or stone-ground yellow cornmeal

4 tablespoons (½ stick) unsalted butter

½ cup freshly grated Parmesan cheese

Braised greens

3 tablespoons olive oil

1 small red onion, halved and thinly sliced

2 garlic cloves, thinly sliced

1¼ pounds mustard greens, ribs removed, leaves chopped

Kosher salt and freshly ground black pepper

2 tablespoons red wine vinegar

4 poached eggs (see page 107)

Chile Oil (recipe opposite)

Chopped fresh flat-leaf parsley

1 // Cook the polenta. Bring 3 cups cold water, the milk, salt, and pepper to a boil in a medium saucepan over high heat. Gradually whisk in the polenta; whisk constantly until the mixture is smooth and begins to thicken, about 5 minutes. Reduce the heat to medium-low and simmer, stirring often, until tender and thickened but still creamy, about 30 minutes, adding more water as needed if the mixture seems too dry. Stir in the butter and Parmesan cheese.

2 // Meanwhile, make the braised greens. Heat the oil in a large high-sided sauté pan over high heat. Add the onion and cook until softened, 4 minutes. Add the garlic and cook, stirring occasionally, until slightly golden brown, about 2 minutes. Add the greens, season with salt and pepper, and toss to coat. Reduce the heat to medium, stir in 1 cup water, cover, and cook until wilted and soft, about 20 minutes. Remove the lid during the last 5 minutes to cook off any additional liquid. Stir in the vinegar just before serving.

3 // To serve, spoon some of the polenta into bowls, top with some of the greens and a poached egg per bowl. Drizzle with the chile oil and garnish with the chopped parsley.

SCRAMBLED EGGS

ON BUTTERMILK BISCUITS
WITH SAUSAGE AND CREAM GRAVY

SERVES 8

At my restaurant Bar Americain, I serve a dish much like this one. It's a menu mainstay, keeping southern transplants, and those Yankees who know a good thing when they taste it, happy.

Gravy

2 cups whole milk

2 tablespoons unsalted butter

2 tablespoons all-purpose flour

1 teaspoon kosher salt

⅛ teaspoon freshly ground black pepper

Pinch of freshly grated nutmeg

Pinch of cayenne pepper

1 tablespoon finely chopped chives, plus more for serving

Scrambled eggs

8 large eggs, lightly beaten

Kosher salt and freshly ground black pepper

6 tablespoons (¾ stick) unsalted butter

Buttermilk Biscuits (page 154)

8 pork sausages or breakfast patties, homemade (page 249) or store-bought

1 // Make the gravy. Pour the milk into a small saucepan and bring to a simmer over medium heat. Melt the butter in a medium saucepan over medium heat, whisk in the flour, and cook for 1 minute, whisking constantly; do not allow the flour to color. Slowly whisk in the warm milk, increase the heat to high, and continue whisking until the sauce begins to thicken and the raw taste of the flour has been cooked out, about 5 minutes. Season with the salt, pepper, nutmeg, and cayenne. Fold in the chives, cover, and keep warm.

2 // Cook the eggs. Beat the eggs in a large bowl and season with salt and pepper. Melt the butter over low heat in a large nonstick skillet. Add the eggs and cook slowly, stirring constantly with a wooden spoon, until soft curds form, about 2 minutes.

3 // To serve, split the biscuits, put a sausage patty on the bottom halves, and drizzle cream gravy on top. Serve the eggs on top of the sausage or on the side, garnished with the chives.

TEXAS EGGS BENEDICT

SERVES 4

If you're calling something "Texas," it had better be *big*, and this version of eggs Benedict is just that! Thickly sliced Texas toast, slathered with garlic butter and grilled until golden brown, is home base for a black bean tomato relish, gorgeous strips of flavorful grilled rib eye, a perfectly poached egg, and a gilding of luscious hollandaise-meets–steak sauce.

1 boneless rib eye, 1½ inches thick

2 tablespoons canola oil

Kosher salt and freshly ground black pepper

3 tablespoons Bobby Flay's Steak Rub for Beef and Pork or your favorite meat rub

6 tablespoons (¾ stick) unsalted butter, softened

2 garlic cloves, smashed to a paste

4 (1-inch-thick) slices Pullman white bread

Black Bean Tomato Relish (see page 129)

4 poached eggs (see page 107)

Steak Sauce Hollandaise (see page 129)

1 // Remove the steak from the refrigerator 30 minutes before grilling. Brush both sides with the oil and season with salt and pepper. Rub one side with the rub.

2 // Heat a grill pan over high heat until smoking. Grill the steak, rub side down, until golden brown and a crust has formed, about 5 minutes. Flip over and continue grilling until cooked to medium, about 7 minutes longer. Remove from the grill, loosely tent with foil, and let rest for 10 minutes before slicing into ½-inch-thick slices.

3 // While the steak is resting, heat the grill pan over medium heat. Stir together the butter and garlic and season with salt and pepper. Spread both sides of the bread with the butter and grill on both sides until lightly golden brown. Keep warm.

4 // Divide the toast among 4 plates and top each with the black bean relish, some sliced steak, an egg, and hollandaise sauce.

BLACK BEAN TOMATO RELISH
SERVES 4

1 (15.5-ounce) can black beans, rinsed well and drained

3 tablespoons finely chopped red onion

1 serrano chile, finely chopped

1 plum tomato, seeded and finely diced

2 tablespoons finely chopped fresh cilantro

Juice of 1 lime

Kosher salt and freshly ground black pepper

Combine all the ingredients in a bowl and season with salt and pepper. Let sit at room temperature for 30 minutes to allow the flavors to meld.

STEAK SAUCE HOLLANDAISE
SERVES 4

3 large egg yolks

1 tablespoon fresh lime juice

12 tablespoons (1½ sticks) unsalted butter, melted until foamy

¼ to ½ cup Bobby Flay's Mesa Steak Sauce or your favorite steak sauce, to taste

1 teaspoon kosher salt

¼ teaspoon freshly ground black pepper

Bring a couple of inches of water to a boil in a medium saucepan. Whisk together the egg yolks and lime juice in a medium stainless-steel bowl and set over the pan of simmering water. Whisk the yolks until pale yellow and fluffy, about 3 minutes. Slowly whisk in the melted butter, a few tablespoons at a time, and whisk until thickened. Remove from the heat and whisk in the steak sauce, salt, and pepper. Serve warm.

CARAMELIZED ONION, SPINACH, AND GRUYÈRE STRATA
WITH SAUTÉED CHERRY TOMATOES

SERVES 8

Strata, a savory bread pudding, is an excellent brunch dish to prepare for a crowd. It's best made in advance, and you serve it family style—no need to be tied to the stove flipping omelets for eight.

6 cups ½-inch cubed day-old French bread (with crust)

2 tablespoons unsalted butter, plus more for the baking dish

1 tablespoon canola oil

2 large Spanish onions, halved and thinly sliced

Kosher salt and freshly ground black pepper

1 tablespoon finely chopped fresh thyme

2 cups grated aged Gruyère cheese

1 (10-ounce) box frozen chopped spinach, thawed and squeezed dry

10 large eggs

3 cups whole milk

1 cup heavy cream

2 teaspoons Dijon mustard

⅛ teaspoon freshly grated nutmeg

Sautéed Cherry Tomatoes (recipe opposite)

1 // Preheat the oven to 325°F.

2 // Put the bread on a baking sheet and toast, stirring once, until lightly golden brown, about 10 minutes. Set aside to cool.

3 // Combine the butter and oil in a large sauté pan over medium heat and cook until it begins to shimmer. Add the onions, toss to coat in the butter, and season with salt and pepper. Cook the onion, stirring occasionally, until golden brown and caramelized, about 30 minutes. Stir in the thyme, remove from the heat, and let cool slightly.

4 // Butter a 9 × 13-inch baking dish. Put the bread cubes in the dish and sprinkle them with 1½ cups of the cheese, the onions, and the spinach. In a large bowl, whisk together the eggs, milk, cream, mustard, 1 teaspoon salt, ½ teaspoon pepper, and the nutmeg. Pour the egg mixture over the bread cubes and press down to make sure the bread is totally submerged. Cover and chill for at least 2 hours and up to 24 hours.

5 // Preheat the oven to 350°F.

6 // Uncover the baking dish and bake until the mixture has puffed up slightly and is golden brown on top, and the strata doesn't shimmy when you shake the pan, 1 hour. Sprinkle the remaining ½ cup cheese over the top during the last 10 minutes of baking. Let cool for 5 minutes before serving large spoonfuls on plates and topping with the sautéed tomatoes.

SAUTÉED CHERRY TOMATOES
SERVES 8

3 tablespoons olive oil

2 pints cherry tomatoes

Kosher salt and freshly ground black pepper

3 tablespoons finely sliced fresh chives

Heat the oil in a large sauté pan over high heat until it begins to shimmer. Add the tomatoes, season with salt and pepper, and cook until the tomatoes soften, 5 to 7 minutes. Remove from the heat and stir in the chives. Serve hot.

BEEF GRILLADES

WITH CHEESY CORN AND SWEET ONION GRITS

SERVES 4 TO 6

This classic New Orleans dish epitomizes Bayou cuisine; it's hearty, spicy, and extremely flavorful. Pounded thin and seared before being doused with a savory slew of peppers, onions, and garlic, an inexpensive round steak is transformed into something tender and beyond tasty.

2 pounds round steak (½ inch thick)

Leaves from 2 sprigs of fresh thyme

2 teaspoons sweet Spanish paprika

1 teaspoon dried oregano

1 teaspoon garlic powder

1 teaspoon onion powder

1 teaspoon New Mexican chile powder

½ teaspoon chile de árbol powder

Kosher salt and freshly ground black pepper

2 cups all-purpose flour

4 tablespoons (½ stick) unsalted butter

4 tablespoons canola oil

2 Vidalia onions, halved and thinly sliced

1 poblano chile, thinly sliced

1 red bell pepper, thinly sliced

2 garlic cloves, thinly sliced

2 cups beef or chicken stock

1 (16-ounce) can diced tomatoes, drained

1 tablespoon pureed canned chipotle in adobo, optional

1 bay leaf

Red wine vinegar

Honey

¼ cup chopped fresh flat-leaf parsley

Cheesy Corn and Sweet Onion Grits (page 238)

4 to 6 poached eggs (see page 107), optional

1 // Preheat the oven to 350°F.

2 // Put the steak between 2 pieces of plastic wrap or wax paper and evenly pound until about ⅛ inch thick. Cut the steak into 2-inch pieces.

3 // Combine the thyme, paprika, oregano, garlic powder, onion powder, and both chile powders in a small bowl.

4 // Season the beef on both sides with salt and pepper. Put the flour in a shallow baking dish and season with salt and pepper. Dredge the beef lightly in the flour, tapping off the excess.

5 // Heat 2 tablespoons of the butter and 2 tablespoons of the canola oil in a large high-sided ovenproof sauté pan over high heat. Add half of the beef and brown, turning once, about 4 minutes. Remove to a plate and repeat with the remaining butter, oil, and beef.

6 // Add the onions, poblano, and red pepper to the pan and cook until soft, about 5 minutes. Add the spice mixture and cook, stirring, for 2 minutes. Add the garlic and cook for 1 minute. Add the stock, tomatoes, chipotle, if using, and bay leaf, bring to a boil, and cook for 5 minutes.

7 // Add the beef, cover the pan, and cook in the oven until tender, about 30 minutes. Remove the beef to a bowl and cover to keep warm.

8 // Using pot holders, put the pan on the stove over high heat and boil, stirring occasionally, until thickened, about 10 minutes. Season with a splash of vinegar, a little honey, and salt and pepper to taste; stir in the parsley. Pour over the beef.

9 // Spoon the grits into bowls and top each serving with beef and sauce and an egg, if desired.

MOROCCAN EGGS

WITH FLATBREAD AND GOAT CHEESE

SERVES 4

Ras el hanout, a signature Moroccan spice blend, combines with smoky paprika and fiery harissa to season a lush tomato bath for spicy merguez sausage. The eggs are poached right in this one-pot wonder, and their buttery yolks and fresh goat cheese mellow all those intensely savory flavors.

At least 4 pieces flatbread, pita, naan, or lavash

6 tablespoons olive oil

¾ pound merguez sausage, casings removed

1 medium Spanish onion, halved and thinly sliced

2 garlic cloves, thinly sliced

1 tablespoon ras el hanout

1 teaspoon sweet smoked Spanish paprika

1 (28-ounce) can plum tomatoes, coarsely crushed with juice

1 to 2 tablespoons harissa, to taste

4 tablespoons coarsely chopped fresh cilantro leaves

4 tablespoons coarsely chopped fresh flat-leaf parsley leaves

Kosher salt and freshly ground black pepper

Touch of honey, optional

8 large eggs

4 ounces soft goat cheese, crumbled

1 // Preheat the oven to 250°F. Wrap the flatbread in foil and place in the oven to warm while you cook the eggs.

2 // Heat a large ovenproof high-sided sauté pan over high heat. Add 2 tablespoons of the oil and heat until it begins to shimmer. Add the sausage and cook, stirring occasionally, until golden brown and just cooked through, about 7 minutes. Remove to a plate lined with paper towels. Wipe out the pan.

3 // Return the pan to high heat and add the remaining 4 tablespoons oil. Add the onion and cook until light golden brown, about 5 minutes. Add the garlic and cook for 1 minute. Add the ras el hanout and paprika and cook for 1 minute.

4 // Add the tomatoes and their juice, 1 cup water, and the harissa, bring to a boil, reduce the heat to medium-low, and simmer until the sauce thickens, about 15 minutes. Stir in 2 tablespoons of the cilantro and 2 tablespoons of the parsley and cook for 1 minute longer. Season with salt and pepper and honey, if needed, to round out the sauce.

5 // Carefully crack the eggs over the mixture and cover with a lid for a few minutes. Remove the lid and continue to cook until the whites are set but the yolks are still runny, 1 or 2 minutes longer. Sprinkle the cheese and remaining 2 tablespoons of each herb over the top and cover for a minute to allow the cheese to warm through.

6 // Bring the pan to the table, scoop 2 eggs and sauce onto each of 4 plates, and serve with the warm flatbread on the side for dipping.

CHILES RELLENOS

WITH MIGAS, PULLED CHICKEN, AND CHEESE SAUCE

SERVES 8

This is a delicious way to share some love and warmth on a cold day. Every last bite—from the tender shreds of chicken and the crisp strips of tortillas to the ooey-gooey cheese sauce and the classic Mexican salsa that grounds it all—is comforting and craveable. Yes, there are a lot of steps here, but none is particularly difficult, and the end result is totally worth your time. (And I would look the other way if you wanted to use a store-bought rotisserie chicken and tortilla chips.)

8 poblano chiles

1 cup plus 5 tablespoons canola oil

2 (6-inch) yellow tortillas

2 (6-inch) blue corn tortillas

Kosher salt and freshly ground black pepper

8 bone-in skinless chicken thighs

2 tablespoons ancho chile powder

2 cups chicken stock

¼ cup Bobby Flay BBQ sauce or your favorite barbecue sauce

1½ cups heavy cream

1½ cups Chihuahua cheese

2 tablespoons unsalted butter

1 small red onion, finely diced

1 medium bell pepper, thinly sliced

1 jalapeño, finely diced

1 large garlic clove, finely chopped

12 large eggs, lightly beaten

1 cup shredded aged white cheddar

¼ cup chopped fresh cilantro leaves, plus more for serving

Cooked Tomato Salsa (recipe opposite)

1 // Preheat the oven to 375°F.

2 // Cut the stems out of the poblanos and discard. Rub the poblanos with 1 tablespoon of the canola oil, put on a baking sheet, and roast in the oven until blistered all over, 20 minutes. Cover and set aside to cool. Carefully remove the seeds and blackened skin while leaving the peppers whole.

3 // Line a baking sheet with paper towels. Heat 1 cup of the oil in a medium high-sided sauté pan over medium heat until it begins to shimmer.

4 // While the oil heats, cut 1 of the yellow and 1 of the blue tortillas into ½-inch strips. Add to the hot oil in batches and fry until just crisp, 20 to 30 seconds. Remove with a slotted spoon to one side of the baking sheet and season with salt.

5 // Thinly slice the remaining yellow and blue tortillas and fry in batches in the hot oil. Remove with a slotted spoon to the other side of baking sheet; season with salt and reserve for garnish.

6 // Decrease the oven temperature to 350°F.

7 // Season the chicken thighs with the ancho powder and salt and pepper. Heat 3 tablespoons of the oil in a medium high-sided ovenproof sauté pan over high heat. Sear the chicken on both sides until golden brown, about 4 minutes per side. Add the chicken stock and barbecue sauce, bring to a simmer, cover, and cook in the oven until fork-tender, 1 hour.

8 // Transfer the chicken to a cutting board, tent loosely with foil, and let rest for 15 minutes. Simmer the cooking liquid on top of the stove until reduced to about ½ cup. Shred the chicken with a fork into bite-sized pieces. Add the chicken to the reduced sauce and toss to coat. Set aside.

9 // Decrease the oven temperature to 300°F.

10 // Put the cream in a small saucepan over medium heat and simmer gently until reduced by half, about 7 minutes; do not boil. Whisk in the Chihuahua cheese until melted and then season with salt and pepper. Cover the cheese sauce and keep warm over very low heat.

11 // Melt the butter and remaining 1 tablespoon oil in a large nonstick sauté pan over medium heat. Add the onion and bell pepper and cook until soft, about 5 minutes. Add the jalapeño and garlic and cook for 1 minute. Add the eggs, season with salt and pepper, and stir with a heatproof silicone spatula until small curds form, about 3 minutes.

Remove from the heat and fold in the cheddar cheese, chicken, ½-inch tortilla strips, and the chopped cilantro. Divide the mixture among the roasted poblanos.

12 // Spoon some of the tomato salsa onto large dinner plates, top each with a stuffed poblano, and drizzle with some of the cheese sauce. Garnish with the thinly sliced fried tortillas and some cilantro leaves.

COOKED TOMATO SALSA
SERVES 8

6 large overly ripe beefsteak tomatoes, halved and seeded

2 jalapeños, chopped

6 garlic cloves, chopped

4 tablespoons canola oil

1 teaspoon dried Mexican oregano

Kosher salt and freshly ground black pepper

1 // Combine the tomatoes, jalapeño, garlic, and 1 cup cold water in a blender and blend until smooth.

2 // Heat the oil in a large sauté pan over medium heat until it just begins to shimmer. Add the pureed tomato mixture, the oregano, and salt and pepper to taste and simmer until the mixture thickens slightly and becomes a deep red, about 15 minutes. Serve hot or warm.

SMOKED SALMON AND GREEN ONION SCRAMBLE

WITH GOAT CHEESE BUTTER ON TOAST

SERVES 4 TO 6

The inspiration behind this dish is old-school New York: picking up smoked salmon from Russ and Daughters on the Lower East Side and serving it with eggs atop a bagel with a schmear of cream cheese and a smattering of chives. I mix the pink flakes of salty, smoky salmon into the eggs and serve them on whole-grain toast slathered with a tangy yet rich blend of goat cheese and butter flecked with green onion.

2 ounces fresh goat cheese

8 tablespoons (1 stick) unsalted butter, at room temperature

Kosher salt and freshly ground black pepper

4 to 6 (½-inch-thick) slices 12-grain bread

8 large eggs

8 ounces smoked wild salmon, flaked

2 large green onions, finely sliced

1 // Stir together the goat cheese and 4 tablespoons of the butter and season with salt and pepper.

2 // Toast the slices of bread. Spread the goat cheese butter over the warm pieces of toast.

3 // Whisk together the eggs until smooth and season with salt and pepper. Melt the remaining 4 tablespoons butter in a large nonstick sauté pan over medium heat until it begins to shimmer. Add the eggs and slowly cook until soft curds form. Remove from the heat and stir in the salmon and green onions. Spoon the eggs over the pieces of toast.

CALABRIAN SCRAMBLED EGGS
WITH JALAPEÑO PESTO BRUSCHETTA

SERVES 6 TO 8

Italy is one of my favorite places to vacation, and every time I return I find myself inspired in the kitchen. This dish would probably not be found on any breakfast menu in Calabria, but the ingredients certainly would. These eggs, loaded with crisp bites of sopressata and melted provolone, and served up on toasty bread with a spicy smear of jalapeño pesto, are how I translate this southern Italian region for the American brunch table.

1 loaf ciabatta, halved lengthwise

6 tablespoons olive oil

Kosher salt and freshly ground black pepper

6-ounce piece sopressata, cut into small dice

1 small red onion, finely diced

9 large eggs

6 ounces provolone, cut into small dice, at room temperature

Roasted Jalapeño Pesto (page 116)

1 // Preheat the oven to 375°F.

2 // Brush the cut sides of the ciabatta with 4 tablespoons of the olive oil and season with salt and pepper. Put on a baking sheet, cut side up, and bake until lightly golden brown, about 5 minutes.

3 // Heat the remaining 2 tablespoons olive oil in a large nonstick sauté pan over medium heat. Add the sopressata and cook until golden brown and crisp, about 5 minutes. Remove to a plate lined with paper towels. Add the onion to the pan and cook until soft, about 4 minutes.

4 // Whisk the eggs in a bowl until light and fluffy, stir in the cheese, and season with salt and pepper. Pour the mixture into the pan and cook, stirring constantly with a heatproof silicone spatula, until soft curds form and the cheese has melted, about 3 minutes.

5 // Divide the eggs between the ciabatta halves. Cut crosswise into 2-inch slices and then top each piece with a dollop of the pesto.

SOUR ORANGE PORK

WITH SWEET POTATO HASH AND SOFRITO HOLLANDAISE

SERVES 8

This dish is a hats-off to the fresh, dynamic flavors of Cuban cuisine. If you can find sour oranges to make the marinade for the pork shoulder, use them, but I find that a combination of sweet orange and tart lime juices delivers a similar result. Country ham adds smoke, as does chipotle in adobo, and a nice salty note to the hash. A silky hollandaise flavored with onion, garlic, and peppers blankets the dish in smooth, savory richness.

Pork

1 bone-in pork shoulder, about 4 pounds, trimmed of excess fat

12 garlic cloves, coarsely chopped

½ cup olive oil

¼ cup plus 2 tablespoons finely chopped fresh oregano

Grated zest of 1 orange

Grated zest of 1 lime

3½ cups fresh orange juice

1¼ cups fresh lime juice

Kosher salt and freshly ground black pepper

2 cups canola oil, optional

1 green plantain, peeled and julienned, optional

Kosher salt and freshly ground black pepper

4 tablespoons (½ stick) unsalted butter

8 large eggs

2 recipes Sweet Potato Hash with Country Ham (page 229)

Sofrito Hollandaise (recipe opposite)

Fresh cilantro leaves

1 // Start the pork. Using a paring knife, make small slits over the entire surface of the pork and rub the garlic into the slashes, reserving 1 tablespoon garlic for the orange glaze. Whisk together the olive oil and ¼ cup of the oregano in a large roasting pan, add the pork, and turn to coat. Cover and let marinate in the refrigerator for at least 8 hours and up to 24 hours.

2 // Combine the orange zest, lime zest, 3 cups of the orange juice, and 1 cup of the lime juice in a large nonreactive saucepan over high heat, bring to a boil, and boil until reduced to 2 cups. Remove from the heat and stir in the remaining ½ cup orange juice, remaining ¼ cup lime juice, reserved 1 teaspoon garlic, and remaining 2 tablespoons oregano. Let the orange glaze cool to room temperature.

3 // Preheat the oven to 425°F. Remove the pork from the refrigerator 30 minutes before roasting.

4 // Season the pork with salt and pepper and roast in the oven for 30 minutes.

5 // Decrease the oven temperature to 350°F and continue roasting the pork for 1½ hours. Continue to roast, basting regularly with the orange glaze, until golden brown and a thermometer inserted into the center reaches 175°F, about 30 minutes more.

6 // Remove the pork from the oven, baste with any remaining glaze, tent loosely, and let rest for 15 minutes before slicing.

7 // If desired, heat the 2 cups oil in a medium saucepan until it reaches 360°F. Fry the plantain, in batches, until golden brown and crisp, about 1 minute. Remove to a plate lined with paper towels. Season with salt.

8 // Divide the butter between 2 large nonstick sauté pans over medium heat and heat until it begins to foam. Carefully crack 4 eggs into each pan, season with salt and pepper, and fry to desired doneness.

9 // Place 1 hash patty on each of 8 plates. Top each hash patty with an egg and some pork, drizzle with the hollandaise, and top with the crisp plantain, if using. Garnish with the cilantro.

SOFRITO HOLLANDAISE
SERVES 8

2 tablespoons canola oil

½ small Spanish onion, finely diced

½ poblano chile, seeded and finely diced

2 garlic cloves, finely chopped

Kosher salt and freshly ground black pepper

3 large egg yolks

1 tablespoon aged sherry vinegar

12 tablespoons (1½ sticks) unsalted butter, melted until foamy

1 // Heat the oil in a small sauté pan over high heat. Add the onion and poblano and cook until soft, about 4 minutes. Add the garlic and cook for 30 seconds. Season with salt and pepper, remove from the heat, and let cool slightly.

2 // Bring a couple of inches of water to a simmer in a large saucepan. Put the egg yolks in a medium stainless-steel bowl, whisk in the vinegar, and set over the pan of simmering water. Whisk the yolks until pale yellow and fluffy, about 3 minutes. Slowly add the melted butter, a few tablespoons at a time, and whisk until thickened. Stir in the onion mixture and season with salt and pepper. Serve immediately or keep warm in a double boiler for up to 15 minutes.

PASTRIES
& BREADS

BLACK PEPPER POPOVERS

MAKES 6 POPOVERS

These billowy, savory popovers are as fantastic alongside a roasted piece of meat as they are served in your brunch bread basket. Their name comes from the way in which the batter pops over the sides of its tin as the hollow, eggy rolls bake; serve them fresh from the oven before they have a chance to fall.

1 tablespoon unsalted butter, melted, plus more for the pan

¾ cup all-purpose flour

½ teaspoon kosher salt

½ teaspoon coarsely ground black pepper

2 large eggs, at room temperature

¾ cup whole milk, at room temperature

1 // Preheat the oven to 425°F.

2 // Generously brush a 6-slot aluminum popover pan with softened butter. Put the pan in the oven to heat for 5 minutes while you make the batter.

3 // Whisk together the flour, salt, pepper, eggs, milk, and melted butter until smooth. The batter will be thin. Fill the popover pan less than half full and bake for exactly 30 minutes. Do not open the oven while the popovers are baking. Remove from the molds and serve immediately.

ASPARAGUS AND CHEESE POPOVER
WITH FONTINA AND SPICY HERB OIL

This spring popover is like a cross between an omelet and a Dutch baby pancake; it emerges from the oven with a puffy crust and golden yellow center. Grassy asparagus and creamy fontina cheese are an awesome pairing, and the bright, just-spicy-enough herbaceous chile oil is truly delicious.

Nonstick cooking spray

½ pound asparagus, bottoms trimmed

4 large eggs

½ cup whole milk, at room temperature

½ cup all-purpose flour

Kosher salt and freshly ground black pepper

1 cup shredded fontina cheese

2 tablespoons unsalted butter

¼ cup freshly grated Parmigiano-Reggiano

Spicy Herb Oil (recipe follows)

1 // Preheat the oven to 425°F. Spray a 12-inch cast-iron skillet with nonstick spray and put the pan in the oven to heat.

2 // Bring a medium skillet of salted water to a boil, add the asparagus, and cook until just tender, about 2 minutes, depending on size. Drain, rinse with cold water, drain well, and dry on a plate lined with paper towels.

3 // Whisk together the eggs and milk until smooth. Slowly whisk in the flour until smooth; season with salt and pepper. Add ½ cup of the fontina.

4 // Using pot holders, carefully remove the pan from the oven, add the butter, and stir until melted. Arrange the asparagus in the pan. Pour the egg mixture on top. Bake until puffed and golden brown, about 15 minutes. Do not open the oven while the popover is cooking.

5 // Remove from the oven, sprinkle the remaining ½ cup fontina and the Parmigiano-Reggiano on top, and return to the oven. Bake for 1 minute, until the cheese has melted. Remove from the oven, drizzle with some of the herb oil, and serve immediately.

SPICY HERB OIL
MAKES ABOUT ½ CUP

½ serrano chile, finely diced

1 tablespoon finely chopped fresh flat-leaf parsley

1 tablespoon finely chopped fresh mint

1 tablespoon finely chopped fresh basil

½ cup extra-virgin olive oil

Kosher salt and freshly ground black pepper

Put the serrano, parsley, mint, and basil in a small bowl. Stir in the olive oil and season with salt and pepper. Let sit at room temperature for at least 30 minutes and up to 2 hours before serving to allow the flavors to meld.

CRUMPETS

WITH WHIPPED BUTTER AND ORANGE-BLUEBERRY MARMALADE

MAKES 8 CRUMPETS

These yeasted griddle cakes, split to reveal the "nooks and crannies" you know so well from store-bought English muffins, taste even better when slathered with homemade butter, easily made in a mixer with the whisk attachment. Orange marmalade is another British teatime staple, and I like mine sweetened with popping fresh blueberries to cut the marmalade's slightly bitter quality.

1¼ cups whole milk, lukewarm

2 tablespoons unsalted butter, melted

1 tablespoon clover honey

3½ cups all-purpose flour

2½ teaspoons instant yeast

1 teaspoon baking powder

½ teaspoon fine sea salt

Nonstick cooking spray

Whipped Butter (page 56)

Orange-Blueberry Marmalade (page 55)

1 // Combine 1¼ cups lukewarm water and the milk, melted butter, honey, flour, yeast, baking powder, and salt in the bowl of a stand mixer and mix with the dough hook attachment on high speed until completely mixed and a soft dough has formed, 2 minutes.

2 // Remove the bowl from the machine, cover the top with a clean cloth or plastic wrap, and put in a warm spot until risen and bubbly, about 1 hour.

3 // Lightly spray a cast-iron or nonstick skillet or griddle with nonstick cooking spray and put over medium heat for 5 minutes. Spray 8 (2½-inch) English muffin or crumpet rings well and put them in the pan or on the griddle.

4 // Fill each ring with a scant ¼ cup of the batter. Cook until the bottoms are lightly golden brown and the crumpet is set, 3 to 5 minutes. Carefully remove the rings, flip the crumpets, and cook until the second side is lightly golden brown and the crumpet is completely cooked through, 3 to 5 minutes longer.

5 // Butter the tops and spread with marmalade or split the crumpets and toast (like you would an English muffin) first, if desired.

ANGEL BISCUITS

MAKES ABOUT 1 DOZEN BISCUITS

Angel biscuits are a cross between a traditional baking powder biscuit and a yeast roll. Though they are historically pure white, I cut the shortening with butter, which adds a touch of golden color along with its rich flavor, while still retaining the heavenly light and fluffy texture.

2½ cups all-purpose flour, plus more for rolling

2 teaspoons instant yeast

2 tablespoons sugar

¾ teaspoon fine sea salt

2½ teaspoons baking powder

¼ cup vegetable shortening

4 tablespoons (½ stick) unsalted butter, cut into pats, cold, plus 4 tablespoons, melted

1 cup whole milk, at room temperature

Nonstick cooking spray

¼ cup heavy cream

1 // Whisk together the flour, yeast, sugar, salt, and baking powder in a large bowl. Cut in the shortening and cold butter using a pastry cutter or 2 knives until pea-sized bits remain. Add the milk and gently stir until combined. The dough will be wet.

2 // Transfer the dough to a well-floured surface and gently pat into a 9-inch round that is 1 inch thick. Cut the dough into 2-inch rounds using a cookie cutter. Transfer the rounds to a baking sheet lined with parchment paper that has been lightly sprayed with cooking spray. Cover with a clean kitchen towel and let sit at room temperature for 1 hour.

3 // Remove the towel, cover with plastic wrap, and freeze for 1 hour and up to 24 hours. The longer the biscuits stay in the freezer, the lighter and fluffier they become.

4 // Preheat the oven to 400°F.

5 // Brush the tops of the biscuits with the cream and then bake until golden brown, about 15 minutes. Remove from the oven and brush the tops with the melted butter. Transfer to a wire rack and let cool slightly before serving warm or at room temperature.

BUTTERMILK BISCUITS

MAKES 8 BISCUITS

Light, fluffy, and so tender, these biscuits are a must-make anytime I am serving brunch at home or in my restaurant Bar Americain, and I wouldn't have it any other way. Covered with sausage and cream gravy (see page 126), or split, buttered, and smeared with jam, this classic southern biscuit does not disappoint.

4 cups all-purpose flour, plus more for shaping

4 teaspoons baking powder

1 teaspoon baking soda

1 teaspoon kosher salt

12 tablespoons (1½ sticks) unsalted butter, cut into small pieces, cold

1½ cups buttermilk, cold

½ cup heavy cream

2 teaspoons freshly ground black pepper

1 // Preheat the oven to 450°F.

2 // Whisk together the flour, baking powder, baking soda, and salt in a large bowl. Cut in the butter using your fingers or a pastry cutter until the mixture resembles coarse meal. Add the buttermilk and gently mix until the mixture just begins to come together.

3 // Scrape the dough onto a lightly floured counter. Pat the dough into a 10 × 12-inch rectangle about ¾ inch thick. Use a 3-inch round cutter to cut out biscuits. Press together the scraps of dough and repeat the process to make 8 biscuits.

4 // Put the biscuits on a baking sheet lined with parchment paper; brush the tops with the cream and sprinkle with the black pepper. Bake until lightly golden brown, 12 to 15 minutes. Cool at least slightly on a baking rack.

BISCUIT STICKY BUNS

These have everything you love about sticky buns—
the sweet caramel glaze, the cinnamon sugar rolled
into every crevice, the crunchy bits of pecans—without
the arduous wait involved with the standard yeasted
version. You can cut two hours from your total time by
subbing in a tender biscuit dough, which means you
can serve these to your brunch guests hot from
the oven without having to wake up at dawn.

Buns

3 tablespoons unsalted butter, at room temperature, plus
more for the pan

Dough for Buttermilk Biscuits (page 154), made without
pepper

All-purpose flour

¼ cup granulated sugar

3 tablespoons light brown sugar

½ teaspoon ground cinnamon

½ cup finely chopped toasted pecans

Topping

6 tablespoons (¾ stick) unsalted butter

1¼ cups packed light brown muscovado sugar

½ cup heavy cream

Pinch of fine sea salt

½ cup coarsely chopped toasted pecans

1 // Preheat the oven to 375°F. Lightly butter
a 9-inch-square baking pan.

2 // Form the buns. Scrape the dough onto a lightly
floured counter. Using a rolling pin, roll the dough
into a 12 × 16-inch rectangle about ¼ inch thick.
Position the dough so the short side is facing you.
Brush the surface of the dough with the butter.
Combine the granulated sugar, brown sugar, and
cinnamon in a small bowl and sprinkle the mixture
evenly over the butter, leaving a ½-inch border.
Scatter the finely chopped pecans over the sugar
mixture. Fold ¼ inch of the short side in, and then
roll the dough up tightly into a log. Pinch the bottom
of the dough to itself to seal and then gently roll
back and forth to make a smooth cylinder shape.
Even the ends by slicing ¼ inch off each side. Cut
the log into 8 equal pieces.

3 // Make the topping. Combine the butter and
¼ cup water in a medium nonstick saucepan over
high heat and cook until the butter is melted. Whisk
in the light brown muscovado sugar and cook until
smooth and bubbly. Reduce the heat to low, whisk
in the heavy cream, and cook for 1 minute. Stir in
the salt and remove from the heat.

4 // Pour the warm topping into the pan. Scatter
the coarsely chopped pecans evenly over the
surface. Put the buns in the pan cut side up. Bake
until puffed and golden brown, 25 to 35 minutes.
Remove from the oven and let cool on a baking
rack for 5 minutes. Carefully invert onto a platter.
Serve warm.

BLACKBERRY-HAZELNUT STICKY BUNS

MAKES 8 BUNS

I have yet to meet a sticky bun I didn't like, and I am especially fond of these purple lacquered beauties, which come together quickly thanks to store-bought puff pastry. Blackberries and hazelnuts, both native to the Pacific Northwest, go so well together and make a nice pairing with cinnamon in these sweet buns.

Topping

- 1 cup fresh or frozen blackberries
- 2 tablespoons granulated sugar
- 1 tablespoon fresh lemon juice
- 5 tablespoons unsalted butter
- ½ cup packed light brown muscovado sugar
- ¾ cup toasted hazelnuts, coarsely chopped

Buns

- All-purpose flour
- ½ (17.3-ounce) package all-butter frozen puff pastry, defrosted
- 4 tablespoons (½ stick) unsalted butter, at room temperature
- 1 pint fresh blackberries, halved
- ⅓ cup granulated sugar
- 2 teaspoons ground cinnamon

1 // Start the topping. Combine the blackberries, granulated sugar, and lemon juice in a small bowl. Let macerate at room temperature for 30 minutes. Mash with a fork, then strain the juice into a small bowl; discard the solids.

2 // Preheat the oven to 375°F. Put a 12-cup standard muffin tin on a baking sheet lined with parchment paper.

3 // Melt the butter in a small saucepan over medium heat. Whisk in the brown sugar and blackberry juice and simmer until the mixture is smooth and slightly thickened, about 5 minutes. Divide the blackberry mixture among 8 of the muffin cups and scatter the hazelnuts on top.

4 // Make the buns. Lightly flour a flat surface. Unfold the sheet of puff pastry onto the floured surface, dust with flour, and lightly roll with a rolling pin to an even thickness. Brush with the butter, leaving a 1-inch border at the edge. Scatter the blackberries over the butter.

5 // Combine the granulated sugar and cinnamon in a small bowl and sprinkle over the blackberries. Starting with a long side, roll the pastry up snugly like a jelly roll around the filling, finishing the roll with the seam side down. Trim the ends of the roll about ½ inch and discard. Slice the roll into 8 equal pieces, each about 1½ inches wide. Place one piece, spiral side up, in each of the prepared muffin cups.

6 // Bake until the sticky buns are golden to dark brown on top and firm to the touch, 30 minutes. Remove the pan from the oven to a baking rack and let sit for 5 minutes. Using oven mitts, carefully turn the rolls upside down onto a platter. Serve warm.

PECAN PIE MONKEY BREAD

SERVES 6 TO 8

It takes serious willpower to stop eating bite after bite of this chewy pecan- and caramel-layered bread.

Dough

1 (¼-ounce) envelope active dry yeast

1¼ cups 2% milk, lukewarm (105° to 110°F)

5½ tablespoons unsalted butter, melted, plus more for the bowl and pan

2 large eggs

¼ cup granulated sugar

1 teaspoon kosher salt

5 cups all-purpose flour

Caramel

⅔ cup packed light brown sugar

4 tablespoons (½ stick) unsalted butter, cubed

¼ cup heavy cream

¾ cup chopped pecans

Topping

1 cup granulated sugar

1 teaspoon ground cinnamon

8 tablespoons (1 stick) unsalted butter, melted

1 // Mix the dough. In the bowl of a stand mixer, dissolve the yeast in ¼ cup lukewarm water; let sit for 5 minutes until foamy. Add the milk, butter, eggs, granulated sugar, salt, and 3 cups of the flour. Attach the dough hook and mix on medium speed for 3 minutes. Stir in enough of the remaining 2 cups flour to form a firm dough.

2 // Turn the dough out onto a floured surface and knead until smooth and elastic, 6 to 8 minutes. Put in a greased bowl, turning once to grease the top. Cover and refrigerate overnight.

3 // The next day, grease a 10-inch fluted tube or Bundt pan with butter.

4 // Make the caramel. In a small saucepan, bring the brown sugar, butter, and cream to a boil over high heat. Cook and stir until slightly dark and thick, about 5 minutes. Pour half of the caramel into the pan and sprinkle with half of the pecans.

5 // Make the topping. In a shallow bowl, combine the granulated sugar and cinnamon. Pour the melted butter into a separate bowl.

6 // Punch down the dough and shape into 40 balls, each about 1¼ inches in diameter. Dip the balls in the butter and then roll in the sugar mixture. Arrange 20 of the balls in the tube pan and then top with the remaining caramel and remaining pecans. Top with the remaining 20 balls. Cover and let rise until doubled in size, about 45 minutes.

7 // Preheat the oven to 350°F.

8 // Bake the bread until golden brown, 30 to 35 minutes. Cover loosely with foil if the top browns too quickly. Let cool for 10 minutes in the pan before inverting onto a serving plate. Serve warm.

GRAPE FOCACCIA

SERVES 6 TO 8; MAKES 2 (9-INCH) FOCACCIA

Once a year, in September, bakeries in Florence give *schiacciata all'uva* the place of honor in their shop windows. Make this chewy flatbread, studded with sweet red grapes, once and you'll be hard pressed to wait a year for a repeat performance! It's perfect for a brunch bread basket while still a little unexpected.

2 tablespoons milk, slightly warmed (105° to 110°F)

2 teaspoons granulated sugar

1¼ teaspoons active dry yeast

2 cups all-purpose flour, plus more for shaping

½ teaspoon fine sea salt

6 tablespoons extra-virgin olive oil, plus more for the bowl and pans

2 cups halved seedless red grapes

¼ cup turbinado sugar

1 teaspoon coarse sea salt

Fresh rosemary leaves

1 // In the bowl of an electric mixer fitted with the paddle attachment, stir together ¾ cup lukewarm water and the milk, granulated sugar, and yeast. Let the mixture sit until foamy, about 10 minutes. Add the flour, fine sea salt, and 2 tablespoons of the olive oil and mix well on low. Attach the dough hook, raise the speed to medium-low, and knead the dough for 8 minutes longer.

2 // Brush a large bowl with olive oil. Scrape the dough into the bowl and brush the top with additional oil. Cover with plastic wrap and let rise in a warm place until the dough doubles in bulk, about 1½ hours.

3 // Gently press the dough down, then turn the dough out onto a floured surface, and divide it into 2 balls. Brush 2 (13 × 18-inch) rimmed baking sheets with olive oil, put a ball of dough on each, and brush the tops with more oil. Cover lightly with a kitchen towel and set aside for 20 minutes.

4 // Dip your fingers in olive oil and press and stretch each ball of dough into an 8- to 9-inch circle. It will be dimpled from your fingers. Cover again with the towel and let it rise in a slightly warm place until doubled in size, 1¼ hours.

5 // Preheat the oven to 450°F.

6 // Brush the tops of the dough with the remaining 4 tablespoons olive oil and sprinkle the grapes, turbinado sugar, coarse sea salt, and rosemary evenly over the dough. Bake until the crust is golden brown and puffed around the edges, 15 minutes. Let cool at least slightly before serving. Serve warm or at room temperature.

BROWNED BUTTER BANANA BREAD

WITH VANILLA BEAN BUTTER

MAKES 1 (9-INCH) LOAF

MAKES 1 (9-INCH) LOAF

Browned butter adds a subtly nutty, toasty flavor to this simple banana bread recipe that tastes anything but. It also results in a moist crumb that you'd otherwise need to use oil to achieve—and believe me, the butter tastes much better!

5 tablespoons unsalted butter, plus more for the pan

1½ cups all-purpose flour

1 teaspoon baking soda

¼ teaspoon kosher salt

⅛ teaspoon ground cinnamon

3 large or 4 medium overly ripe bananas (skins should be black), peeled and halved

½ cup sugar

2 tablespoons clover honey

1 large egg, beaten

1 cup fresh blueberries or chopped peaches or nectarines, optional

½ cup chopped pecans or walnuts, optional

Vanilla Bean Butter (page 60)

1 // Preheat the oven to 350°F. Butter a 9-inch loaf pan.

2 // Put the butter in a small saucepan over medium heat and cook until the butter turns a deep golden brown color, about 5 minutes. Set aside to cool slightly.

3 // Sift the flour, baking soda, salt, and cinnamon into a small bowl.

4 // Mash the bananas in a medium bowl (using a potato masher or fork) until smooth. Whisk in the sugar, browned butter, honey, and egg. Add the flour mixture and whisk until just combined; do not overmix. Fold in the blueberries and nuts, if using.

5 // Scrape the batter into the prepared pan and bake on the lower rack of the oven until a toothpick inserted into the center comes out clean, 40 to 50 minutes. Let cool on a baking rack in the pan for 15 minutes. Remove from the pan and let cool on the rack for at least 30 minutes before slicing. Serve with the vanilla bean butter.

ORANGE FRENCH YOGURT CAKE

WITH MARMALADE GLAZE

This lovely moist cake has a texture somewhere between a muffin and a loaf cake, or quick bread. Traditionally, the cake's ingredients were all measured using the empty yogurt container as a guide; I love the history, but I'm sticking with the cups and teaspoons I'm familiar with! A simple glaze of bright orange marmalade and Grand Marnier reinforces the delicate orange flavor of the zest in the batter.

4 tablespoons (½ stick) unsalted butter, melted and cooled slightly, plus more for the pan

1½ cups all-purpose flour

2 teaspoons baking powder

¼ teaspoon fine sea salt

1 cup plain whole milk Greek yogurt

1 cup sugar

3 large eggs

2 teaspoons grated orange zest

½ teaspoon pure vanilla extract

¼ cup canola oil

¼ cup orange marmalade

1 tablespoon Grand Marnier

1 // Preheat the oven to 350°F. Butter an 8½ × 4¼-inch light-colored loaf pan.

2 // Sift the flour, baking powder, and salt into a medium bowl. Combine the yogurt, sugar, eggs, orange zest, vanilla, butter, and oil in a large bowl and whisk until well blended. Gradually whisk in the flour mixture. Transfer the batter to the prepared pan.

3 // Put the pan on a baking sheet and bake on the middle rack of the oven until the cake begins to pull away from the sides of the pan and a tester inserted into the center comes out with a few moist crumbs attached, about 50 minutes. Cool the cake in the pan on a rack for 5 minutes. Cut around the edges of the pan to loosen the cake. Turn the cake out onto the rack, turn upright, and let cool completely.

4 // Stir the marmalade and Grand Marnier together in a small saucepan over medium heat until the marmalade melts. Brush the hot mixture over the top of the cake. Let the glaze cool and set before cutting the cake into slices and serving.

BEIGNETS
WITH QUICK HOMEMADE BERRY JAM

SERVES 8; MAKES ABOUT 4 DOZEN BEIGNETS

Beignets are deliciously light and airy rounds of fried yeasted dough—kind of like the best hole-less doughnut you ever had. Originally brought to the States by the French, they are a New Orleans specialty. I serve them on the brunch menu at Bar Americain, and they are a really great way to start a special day.

1 (¼-ounce) envelope active dry yeast

¼ cup granulated sugar

¾ teaspoon fine sea salt

½ teaspoon freshly grated nutmeg

1 large egg

½ cup whole milk

1 teaspoon grated lemon zest

3½ cups all-purpose flour, plus more for sprinkling

2 tablespoons unsalted butter, softened

2 quarts canola oil, plus more for the bowl

Confectioners' sugar

Quick Homemade Berry Jam (page 53)

1 // Mix the yeast, ¾ cup lukewarm water, and the granulated sugar in the bowl of a stand mixer fitted with the dough hook attachment. Let stand until foamy, about 5 minutes. Add the salt, nutmeg, egg, milk, lemon zest, and 1½ cups of the flour. Mix on medium speed until combined. Add the butter and mix until incorporated. Add 1¾ cups of the flour and mix until the dough comes together.

2 // Turn out the dough onto a lightly floured surface. Knead in the remaining ¼ cup flour by hand until the dough is smooth, about 5 minutes. Put the dough in a lightly oiled bowl, cover loosely with plastic wrap, and let stand in a warm, draft-free spot until doubled in size, about 1 hour.

3 // Punch down the dough and then turn out onto a lightly floured surface. Roll until ½ inch thick. Cut out circles with a 2-inch round cutter and transfer to a floured baking sheet. Let rise in a warm, draft-free spot for 30 minutes.

4 // Heat the oil in a medium pot or deep fryer until it reaches 350°F on a deep-fry thermometer. Fry the beignets in batches, rolling them around constantly with a slotted spoon, until golden brown all over, 1 to 2 minutes. Transfer the beignets with a slotted spoon to a platter lined with paper towels and dust with confectioners' sugar. Serve warm with the berry jam.

BANANAS FOSTER BEIGNETS

WITH CAFÉ BRULOT CRÈME ANGLAISE

SERVES 6; MAKES ABOUT 30 BEIGNETS

Bananas Foster, first made famous at Brennan's in New Orleans's French Quarter in the 1950s, brings its deep brown sugar and ripe banana flavors to these fritter-like beignets. Sprinkled with confectioners' sugar, the beignets could stand on their own, but I like to serve them with a rich crème anglaise that brings to mind one of the city's other signature dishes: the brandy-, clove-, and cinnamon-laced coffee drink known as café brulot.

3 very ripe bananas

2 teaspoons banana liqueur

1 teaspoon pure vanilla extract

¼ cup granulated sugar

2 tablespoons light brown muscovado sugar

1½ cups all-purpose flour

¾ teaspoon baking powder

¾ teaspoon ground cinnamon

Pinch of freshly grated nutmeg

2 to 4 tablespoons whole milk, as needed

Canola oil, for frying

Confectioners' sugar

Café Brulot Crème Anglaise (recipe opposite)

1 // Using a potato masher or large fork, mash the bananas in a large bowl. Mix in the liqueur, vanilla, and both types of sugar.

2 // In another bowl, mix the flour, baking powder, cinnamon, and nutmeg. Add to the banana mixture and pour in 2 tablespoons of the milk. Mix until smooth and thick, like waffle batter, adding a little more milk if needed. Set aside to rest for at least 10 minutes or up to 1 hour.

3 // Heat 2 to 3 inches of canola oil in a heavy pot over medium heat to 350°F on a deep-fry thermometer. Drop the batter by heaping teaspoonfuls into the oil and fry, turning once when the edges are firm, until golden brown on both sides. Drain on paper towels and dust lightly with confectioners' sugar.

4 // Serve immediately, or keep warm in a 200°F oven for up to 2 hours. Sprinkle again with confectioners' sugar just before serving with the crème anglaise.

CAFÉ BRULOT CRÈME ANGLAISE
MAKES ABOUT 3 CUPS

2¼ cups half-and-half or whole milk (depending on how rich you like it)

½ cup chicory coffee beans, coarsely ground

6 whole cloves

1 cinnamon stick

⅓ cup sugar

4 large egg yolks, at room temperature

2 tablespoons brandy

1 teaspoon grated orange zest

1 // Combine the half-and-half, ground coffee beans, cloves, and cinnamon in a medium saucepan and bring to a simmer. Remove from the heat, cover, and refrigerate for at least 1 hour and up to 24 hours.

2 // Strain the mixture through a fine-mesh strainer into a clean small saucepan, add the sugar, and bring to a simmer over medium heat. Discard the solids.

3 // Set a glass or stainless-steel bowl in an ice bath. Whisk the yolks until very pale and thick in a separate bowl. Slowly whisk in some of the hot half-and-half and then return the entire mixture to the pan. Switch to a wooden spoon and stir constantly until the mixture coats the back of the spoon, about 5 minutes. Remove from the heat, add the brandy and orange zest, and pour into the bowl set in the ice bath. Stir until cool. Cover and refrigerate until cold, at least 1 hour, or up to 24 hours.

LEMON RICOTTA FRITTERS

WITH STRAWBERRY JAM

SERVES 6; MAKES ABOUT 3 DOZEN FRITTERS

I make these light, lemony fritters with homemade sweet berry jam for breakfast or brunch on weekends when I am feeling especially hospitable. Both require a bit of extra work, but seeing my friends' and family's reactions when they bite into one of these deep-fried lemony puffs of deliciousness makes it all worthwhile.

Canola oil, for frying

¾ cup all-purpose flour

2 teaspoons baking powder

1 teaspoon grated lemon zest

¼ teaspoon fine sea salt

1 cup whole milk ricotta

2 large eggs

3 tablespoons granulated sugar

1½ teaspoons pure vanilla extract

Confectioners' sugar

Quick Homemade Berry Jam (page 53), made with strawberries

1 // Heat 2 inches of canola oil in a large, wide, heavy saucepan until it reaches 370°F on a deep-fry thermometer.

2 // Whisk together the flour, baking powder, lemon zest, and salt in a bowl. Whisk together the ricotta, eggs, granulated sugar, and vanilla in another bowl. Whisk the ricotta mixture into the flour mixture.

3 // Working in batches, gently drop in tablespoons of batter and fry, turning occasionally, until deep golden, about 3 minutes per batch. Transfer with a slotted spoon to paper towels to drain. Dust generously with confectioners' sugar and serve with the berry jam.

CHURROS

WITH SPICED SUGAR AND CHOCOLATE DIPPING SAUCE

SERVES 4 TO 6; MAKES ABOUT 24 CHURROS

A classic south-of-the-border treat, these doughnut-like pastries are worth the additional effort it may take to find your pastry bag and perfect your deep-frying technique. One bite of golden brown churro, dusted with cinnamon and anise-scented sugar and dipped in a rich chocolate sauce, and there is no question that your efforts will be appreciated.

1 quart canola oil

8 tablespoons (1 stick) unsalted butter, cut into pieces

1¼ cups sugar

¼ teaspoon fine sea salt

1¼ cups all-purpose flour

¾ teaspoon ground cinnamon

¾ teaspoon ground anise seeds

3 large eggs

½ teaspoon pure vanilla extract

Chocolate Dipping Sauce (recipe opposite)

1 // Put the oil into a large saucepan and heat over medium heat until it reaches 365°F on a deep-fry thermometer. Put several layers of paper towels on a baking sheet and set aside.

2 // Combine 1 cup water, the butter, ¼ cup of the sugar, and the salt in a medium saucepan over high heat. Bring to a boil and cook until the butter is completely melted and the sugar is dissolved. Add the flour, ¼ teaspoon of the cinnamon, and ¼ teaspoon of the anise and quickly beat with a wooden spoon until a ball forms and the mixture dries out a little, about 2 minutes.

3 // Transfer the mixture to the bowl of a stand mixer fitted with the paddle attachment and beat for 1 minute to allow some of the steam to escape the mixture and to cool slightly. Add the eggs, one at a time, beating well until each is incorporated before adding the next. Add the vanilla and beat for 20 seconds longer. Scrape the mixture into a pastry bag fitted with a large star tip.

4 // Combine the remaining 1 cup sugar, ½ teaspoon cinnamon, and ½ teaspoon anise in a baking dish.

5 // Working in batches, pipe 6-inch strips of the dough into the hot oil and fry until golden brown, turning once. Remove with a slotted spoon to the baking sheet. Let drain for 30 seconds and then toss in the sugar mixture. Serve warm with the chocolate dipping sauce on the side.

CHOCOLATE DIPPING SAUCE
SERVES 4 TO 6

2 cups whole milk

1 cup heavy cream

2 tablespoons sugar

½ vanilla bean, split lengthwise, seeds scraped

1 pound bittersweet chocolate (66% cacao), coarsely chopped

Combine the milk, cream, sugar, and vanilla bean and seeds in a medium saucepan, bring to a simmer over medium-high heat, and cook until the sugar is completely dissolved, about 1 minute. Remove from the heat, add the chocolate, and let sit for 30 seconds before whisking until smooth. Discard the vanilla bean. Serve warm.

MINI PUMPKIN CHURROS

WITH CHOCOLATE-ORANGE DIPPING SAUCE

SERVES 6; MAKES 32 MINI CHURROS

Churros are fried dough popular in Spain and much of Latin America. You often find them dusted with cinnamon-sugar and served alongside café con leche or my favorite, a rich hot chocolate. Here I add pumpkin to the batter and spike the chocolate dipping sauce with orange for a treat that's perfect for a Mexican Day of the Dead or Halloween celebration—or any fall morning.

2 cups all-purpose flour

2½ teaspoons ground cinnamon

¼ teaspoon ground cloves

¼ teaspoon ground ginger

⅛ teaspoon freshly grated nutmeg

⅛ teaspoon fine sea salt

¾ cup canned pure pumpkin puree

10 tablespoons (1¼ sticks) unsalted butter, cut into pieces

½ teaspoon pure vanilla extract

4 large eggs, at room temperature

¾ cup sugar

Vegetable or canola oil, for frying

Chocolate-Orange Dipping Sauce (recipe opposite)

1 // Whisk together the flour, 1 teaspoon of the cinnamon, the cloves, ginger, nutmeg, and salt in a large bowl.

2 // Bring 1½ cups water, the pumpkin puree, butter, and vanilla to a boil in a medium saucepan, whisking constantly. Pour the pumpkin mixture into the flour mixture and mix with a wooden spoon until just combined; the batter will be thick. Continue mixing and add the eggs, one at a time. The dough will be thick and smooth. Put the dough into a pastry bag fitted with a large star tip.

3 // Stir together the sugar with the remaining 1½ teaspoons cinnamon in a baking dish. Line a baking sheet with paper towels.

4 // Heat 2 inches of oil in a high-sided sauté pan until it reaches 350°F on a deep-fry thermometer. Working in batches, pipe the dough directly into the pan in 3-inch pieces, cutting off the pieces with scissors. Fry, turning as needed, until golden and crisp, 4 to 5 minutes. Remove the churros from the oil and transfer them to the baking sheet to drain for 30 seconds. Toss in the cinnamon-sugar. Serve hot with the dipping sauce.

CHOCOLATE-ORANGE DIPPING SAUCE
MAKES ABOUT 2 CUPS

1 cup heavy cream
Zest of 1 orange, removed with a vegetable peeler
7 ounces bittersweet chocolate, coarsely chopped
1 teaspoon grated orange zest

1 // Combine the heavy cream and strips of zest in a small saucepan, bring to a simmer, remove from the heat, and let steep for 15 minutes.

2 // Discard the strips of zest, return the pan to medium heat, and bring to a simmer. Put the chocolate in a medium bowl, add the hot cream, and let sit for 1 minute. Slowly whisk until smooth; whisk in the grated zest. Serve warm.

SHOOFLY MUFFINS

MAKES 1 DOZEN MUFFINS

A traditional Dutch-Amish recipe that was also adopted by southern cooks, shoofly pie is loaded with gooey, rich molasses and plenty of sweet brown sugar—ingredients as tempting to the flies that need to be shooed away as they are to the rest of us. These muffins are full of the same appealing, deep flavors. A small amount of canola oil ensures a moist crumb, while the butter is what you'll taste.

Nonstick cooking spray

2 cups all-purpose flour

1 cup packed light brown muscovado sugar

Pinch of ground allspice

⅛ teaspoon fine sea salt

6 tablespoons (¾ stick) unsalted butter, cut into pieces, cold

1 teaspoon baking soda

2 tablespoons canola oil

½ cup molasses

½ teaspoon pure vanilla extract

1 // Preheat the oven to 350°F. Line a 12-cup muffin tin with paper baking cups and spray the papers with nonstick cooking spray.

2 // Bring 1 cup water to a boil. In a large bowl, combine the flour, brown sugar, allspice, and salt. Cut in the butter using a pastry cutter or 2 knives until crumbly. Set aside ½ cup for the topping. Add the baking soda to the remaining crumb mixture. Stir in the boiling water, oil, molasses, and vanilla.

3 // Fill the muffin cups two-thirds full with batter. Sprinkle with the reserved crumb mixture. Bake until a toothpick inserted into the center comes out clean, 20 to 25 minutes. Let cool for 10 minutes before removing from the pans to wire racks to cool.

PUMPKIN-CRANBERRY SCONES
WITH WHIPPED MAPLE BUTTER

MAKES 8 SCONES

These scones are as New England as they come, and are a delicious way to bring the stars of your Thanksgiving to the brunch table. These pumpkin scones, studded with sweet-tart dried cranberries and spicy bits of candied ginger, can—and should—be enjoyed year-round, countrywide.

2 cups all-purpose flour, plus more for shaping

1/3 cup lightly packed light brown muscovado sugar

3/4 teaspoon ground cinnamon

1/2 teaspoon ground ginger

1 teaspoon baking powder

1/2 teaspoon baking soda

1/4 teaspoon fine sea salt

8 tablespoons (1 stick) unsalted butter, cut into pieces, cold

1/3 cup buttermilk, or more if needed, very cold

1/2 cup canned pure pumpkin puree

1 teaspoon pure vanilla extract

1/2 cup dried cranberries, soaked in hot water for 30 minutes and drained well

Scant 1/4 cup finely diced candied ginger

1/4 cup heavy cream

Whipped Maple Butter (page 56)

1 // Preheat the oven to 375°F and line a baking sheet with parchment paper.

2 // Whisk together the flour, sugar, cinnamon, ground ginger, baking powder, baking soda, and salt in a large bowl. Cut the butter into the mixture using a pastry cutter or 2 knives until it resembles coarse meal.

3 // Whisk together the buttermilk, pumpkin, and vanilla in a medium bowl until smooth. Add to the flour mixture along with the cranberries and candied ginger and mix until just combined. Add a tablespoon or two more of buttermilk if the batter will not come together but take care not to overmix or the scones will be tough.

4 // Transfer to a lightly floured surface and knead the dough gently four or five times to combine and then pat the dough into a circle that is about 8 inches in diameter and 1½ inches thick. Cut the circle in half, then cut each half into 4 pie-shaped wedges. Put the scones on the baking sheet, leaving space between them. Brush the tops of the scones with the cream.

5 // Bake until golden brown and a toothpick inserted into the middle comes out with a few moist crumbs attached, 20 minutes. Transfer to a rack to cool for at least 15 minutes before serving warm or at room temperature, accompanied by the maple butter.

FRUIT-FILLED MINI "TOASTER" PASTRIES

MAKES 15 OR 16 MINI PASTRIES

I'm sure you're all familiar with the big brand-name item that inspired these tasty bites, and if you didn't grow up eating them, I bet the commercials made you want to! Trust me, the real deal is so much better. Sweet, delectable, jammy berries encased in flaky, buttery pastry . . . oh yeah, these are so good they almost deserve to be in the dessert category. I bake these in the oven and use a toaster oven to reheat any leftovers.

Dough

- 1 tablespoon apple cider vinegar
- 2 cups all-purpose flour, plus more for rolling
- 1 tablespoon granulated sugar
- ⅛ teaspoon fine sea salt
- 10 tablespoons (1¼ sticks) unsalted butter, cut into small pieces, cold

Fruit

- 2 cups quartered fresh strawberries, raspberries, or blackberries
- 2 to 4 tablespoons granulated sugar, depending on sweetness of fruit
- 1 tablespoon fresh lemon juice
- 1 teaspoon cornstarch
- 2 tablespoons strawberry, raspberry, or blackberry jam

- 1 large egg, beaten with 1 tablespoon water
- ½ cup milk
- Confectioners' sugar

1 // Make the dough. Mix together 5 tablespoons cold water and the vinegar in a measuring cup and keep cold.

2 // Combine the flour, granulated sugar, and salt in the bowl of a food processor and pulse a few times to combine. Scatter the cold butter over the top and then pulse a few times until the mixture resembles coarse meal. Add the vinegar mixture a few tablespoons at a time and pulse until the dough just comes together. Transfer to a lightly floured surface and knead gently until the dough just comes together. Form into a disk, cover with plastic wrap, and refrigerate for at least 1 hour and up to 48 hours.

3 // While the dough is chilling, cook the fruit. Combine the berries and granulated sugar in a small saucepan and cook over high heat until the mixture comes to a boil, the fruit starts to break down, and the juices start to release, about 8 minutes. Stir together the lemon juice and cornstarch until combined, add to the boiling fruit, and cook until the mixture begins to thicken, about 1 minute. Stir in the jam. Transfer to a bowl and refrigerate until cold.

4 // Preheat the oven to 375°F. Line baking sheets with parchment paper.

5 // On a lightly floured work surface, roll half of the dough out into a large rectangle that's just larger than 9 × 8 inches and is ⅛ inch thick. Trim the sides with a knife so that you have a 9 × 8-inch rectangle with straight edges. Cut the rectangle into thirds lengthwise so that you have three 3-inch strips. Then cut the strips into fourths so that you have 12 small 3 × 2-inch rectangles total. Carefully transfer these rectangles to one of the prepared baking sheets. Repeat with the other half of the dough. Gather the scraps of both halves and reroll to create more rectangles; you will get 6 to 8 more.

6 // Spoon a heaping teaspoon of fruit filling in the center of half of the rectangles so that it is slightly heaped; do not spread it out. Make sure not to overfill them and to leave about ¼-inch border all around. Brush the border with the egg wash. Lay another rectangle of dough over each fruit-filled piece and press gently around the edges to seal slightly. Use the tines of a fork to press the two layers of dough together and seal completely. Put the baking sheet in the fridge until the pastries are chilled, about 20 minutes.

7 // Lightly brush the tops of the pastries with the milk. Use a toothpick to poke 8 holes over the top surface of each pastry to allow the steam to escape during baking. Bake until golden around the edges, 15 to 20 minutes. Transfer to a wire rack to cool. Sprinkle with confectioners' sugar before serving.

SANDWICHES

FIG JAM, HAM, AND CHEESE PANINI

SERVES 2 TO 4
This panini is a lesson in restraint. Sweet fig jam, thin slices of salty prosciutto or Serrano ham, peppery arugula, and creamy, slightly tangy, grassy Point Reyes Toma cheese (a particular favorite of mine from the West Coast, though a young Asiago or other melting cheese would certainly work) play together in perfect harmony.

1 day-old loaf ciabatta, halved lengthwise

1 cup good-quality fig jam

2 ounces Point Reyes Toma or fontina cheese, grated (½ cup)

Freshly ground black pepper

8 thin slices prosciutto or Serrano ham

1 cup baby arugula

Olive oil

1 // Heat a panini press or cast-iron pan over medium heat.

2 // Spread each side of the bread with some of the fig jam. Top the bottom piece of bread with half of the cheese and season with pepper. Add several slices of ham and some arugula, top with the remaining cheese, and invert the jam-spread top bread on top. Brush the top and bottom of the sandwich with a little oil and press in the panini maker until lightly golden brown and the cheese has melted, or heat in the pan, topping with a weight and flipping once.

3 // Slice the panini in half or quarters and serve.

CROQUE MADAME

A French bistro classic, this grilled ham and cheese dish is rich, comforting, and delicious. Topped with cheesy béchamel sauce that's broiled until golden and bubbly, the sandwich is then crowned with a fried egg (leave off the egg and you have a classic Croque Monsieur).

7 tablespoons unsalted butter

3 tablespoons all-purpose flour

2 cups whole milk, warm

3 cups grated Gruyère cheese (12 ounces)

½ cup freshly grated Parmesan cheese

Kosher salt and freshly ground black pepper

Freshly grated nutmeg

12 (¾-inch-thick) slices white Pullman bread, lightly toasted

6 tablespoons Dijon mustard

12 thin slices baked ham

6 large eggs

1 // Heat 3 tablespoons of the butter in a 2-quart saucepan over medium-high heat. Add the flour and cook, whisking, until smooth, about 1 minute. Whisk in the milk and bring to a boil. Reduce the heat to medium-low and let simmer until slightly reduced and thickened, 6 to 8 minutes. Add ½ cup of the grated Gruyère and the Parmesan and whisk until smooth; season the béchamel sauce with salt, pepper, and nutmeg.

2 // Heat the broiler.

3 // Put 6 slices of the bread on a baking sheet and spread 1 tablespoon mustard over each. Top each with 2 slices ham and then distribute the remaining 2½ cups Gruyère over the ham. Broil until the cheese begins to melt, about 1½ minutes. Top with the remaining 6 bread slices and then pour a generous amount of béchamel on top of each sandwich. Broil until the cheese sauce is bubbling and evenly browned, 2 to 3 minutes.

4 // Meanwhile, melt 2 tablespoons of the butter in a 12-inch nonstick skillet over medium heat. Add 3 of the eggs, season with salt and pepper, and cook until the whites are set but the yolks are still runny. Transfer to a warm plate and then repeat with the remaining butter and eggs.

5 // Serve each sandwich topped with a fried egg.

BACON AND HASH BROWN "QUESADILLA"
WITH EGGS

SERVES 4

I have always made my quesadillas by layering the ingredients with tortillas and baking them, rather than pan-frying. I find the resulting quesadilla to be far lighter, crisper, and suitable for overstuffing—such as here, with smoky bacon and crispy shreds of hash brown potatoes. Add a fried egg and a smattering of fresh tomato salsa, and you've got the best Mexican breakfast sandwich.

2 large russet potatoes (2 pounds), scrubbed

Kosher salt and freshly ground black pepper

4 tablespoons canola oil, plus more for brushing

2 large Spanish onions, halved and thinly sliced

1 poblano chile, roasted (see page 136) and finely diced

1 tablespoon plus 2 teaspoons ancho chile powder

⅓ pound thick-cut bacon, diced

12 (6-inch) flour tortillas

2½ cups grated Monterey Jack cheese

2 tablespoons unsalted butter

4 large eggs

Fresh Tomato Salsa (page 188)

2 tablespoons finely chopped fresh chives

continues

1 // Put the potatoes in a saucepan, add enough cold water to cover by 2 inches, salt the water, and bring to a boil over high heat. Boil until cooked three-quarters of the way through, or not quite tender when pierced with a knife, 15 to 20 minutes. Drain, let cool slightly, peel, and then grate using the large holes of a box grater.

2 // Preheat the oven to 425°F.

3 // Heat 2 tablespoons of the oil in a large sauté pan over medium heat. Add the onions, season with salt and pepper, and cook, stirring occasionally, until golden brown and caramelized, about 30 minutes.

4 // Heat the remaining 2 tablespoons oil in a large nonstick sauté pan over high heat, add the potatoes, and cook until golden brown. Stir in the onions, poblano, and 1 tablespoon of the ancho powder, season with salt and pepper, and cook until just warmed through, about 2 minutes.

5 // Cook the bacon in a skillet over medium heat until browned and crisp, about 8 minutes. Scoop out and transfer to a plate lined with paper towels to drain.

6 // Lay out 8 of the tortillas on a work surface. Divide the hash browns, bacon, and cheese among the tortillas. Stack half of the tortillas on top of the remaining topped ones to create 4 double stacks. Top each with one of the remaining 4 tortillas. Brush the tops with a little oil and sprinkle with the remaining 2 teaspoons ancho powder.

7 // Transfer the quesadillas to a large baking sheet and bake until golden brown and the cheese has melted, 8 to 10 minutes.

8 // When the quesadillas are nearly ready, melt the butter in a large nonstick sauté pan over medium heat. Carefully crack the eggs into the pan, season with salt and pepper, and cook until the whites are set but the yolks are still runny, about 2 minutes.

9 // Top each quesadilla with a fried egg, some of the tomato salsa, and a sprinkling of chives.

FRESH TOMATO SALSA
SERVES 4

2 ripe beefsteak tomatoes or 4 ripe plum tomatoes, diced

½ red onion, halved and thinly sliced

1 jalapeño, finely diced

2 tablespoons fresh lime juice

2 tablespoons canola oil

2 teaspoons honey

2 tablespoons finely chopped fresh cilantro

Kosher salt and freshly ground black pepper

Combine all of the ingredients in a bowl and let sit at room temperature for at least 15 minutes before serving.

MAPLE-ROASTED APPLE AND BRIE PANINI

ON CINNAMON RAISIN BREAD

SERVES 4

This grown-up grilled cheese is elegant enough for entertaining, but easy and comforting enough to make for yourself anytime. Rich, creamy Brie melts beautifully and has just enough bite to stand up to the maple-sweet apples. A smattering of chopped and toasted pecans adds welcome crunch to the panini.

1 Gala apple, halved, cored, and sliced ¼ inch thick

1 Granny Smith apple, halved, cored, and sliced ¼ inch thick

2 tablespoons unsalted butter, melted, plus softened butter for cooking

2 tablespoons pure grade B maple syrup

Squeeze of lemon juice

16 ounces French Brie, thinly sliced (with rind)

8 slices day-old good-quality cinnamon raisin bread

½ cup coarsely chopped toasted pecans

1 // Preheat the oven to 375°F.

2 // Put the Gala and Granny Smith apples in a bowl, add the melted butter, maple syrup, and lemon juice, and toss to coat. Spread the apples on a baking sheet and roast, turning once or twice, until softened and slightly caramelized, about 15 minutes.

3 // Heat a panini press or cast-iron pan over medium heat.

4 // Divide half of the cheese among 4 slices of the bread, add the apples and pecans, and top with the remaining cheese. Top each with one of the remaining slices of bread. Spread the softened butter over the top and bottom of each sandwich and press in the panini maker until lightly golden brown and the cheese has melted, or heat in the pan, topping with a weight and flipping once.

5 // Slice in half and serve.

APPLE, CHEDDAR, AND TURKEY BACON

CORNMEAL WAFFLE SANDWICHES

SERVES 6; MAKES 3 SANDWICHES

A nutty, tender cornmeal waffle studded with shards of crisp turkey bacon makes an amazing "bread" for filling with sweet-tart Granny Smith apple slices, sharp cheddar cheese, and a smear of maple syrup–sweetened Dijon mustard.

1 cup all-purpose flour

1 cup white cornmeal

2 teaspoons baking powder

½ teaspoon baking soda

2 cups buttermilk

5 tablespoons unsalted butter, melted

¼ cup plus 2 tablespoons pure grade B maple syrup

2 large egg yolks

5 slices turkey bacon, cooked until crisp and crumbled into small pieces

2 large egg whites, beaten to stiff peaks

Nonstick cooking spray

¼ cup Dijon mustard

1¼ cups grated sharp cheddar cheese

1 large Granny Smith apple, halved, cored, and thinly sliced

1 // Preheat the oven to 300°F.

2 // Whisk together the flour, cornmeal, baking powder, and baking soda in a medium bowl. Whisk together the buttermilk, butter, ¼ cup of the maple syrup, and the egg yolks in a separate bowl until combined. Add to the flour mixture along with the bacon and stir until just combined. Fold in the egg whites until just combined.

3 // Heat a waffle iron according to the manufacturer's directions. Spray the grates of the waffle iron with nonstick spray, use a scant ½ cup of the batter per grid, close the cover, and cook until golden brown, about 4 minutes, or until steam stops emerging from the waffle iron. The recipe will make 6 waffles.

4 // Whisk together the mustard and remaining 2 tablespoons maple syrup in a small bowl. Put the waffles on a large baking sheet and spread some of the mustard over the tops of each waffle. Sprinkle half of the cheese evenly over 3 of the waffles, arrange the apple slices evenly over the cheese, and then top with the remaining cheese. Put the remaining 3 waffles on top, mustard side down, and transfer to the oven to melt the cheese, about 5 minutes. Slice in half and serve.

OPEN-FACED EGG SALAD TEA SANDWICHES

WITH CRAB AND POPPY SEEDS

SERVES 6 TO 9

Sweet lump crabmeat, feathery dill, and nutty, blue-black poppy seeds make this egg salad one of the tastiest, and loveliest, you've ever seen. Piled on dark pumpernickel cocktail bread, this is a dish that could transition well from the brunch table—I love it as part of an English-style tea—to the cocktail tray.

½ cup mayonnaise, plus more if needed

¼ cup finely diced radish

2 tablespoons Dijon mustard

2 teaspoons white wine vinegar

1 teaspoon smoked Spanish paprika

¼ cup finely chopped fresh dill, plus whole fronds for serving

1 teaspoon black poppy seeds

12 hard-boiled eggs, peeled and finely chopped

6 ounces jumbo lump crabmeat, picked over for shells

Kosher salt and freshly ground black pepper

18 slices cocktail-size pumpernickel bread, lightly toasted and buttered

1 // Whisk together the mayonnaise, radish, mustard, vinegar, paprika, chopped dill, and poppy seeds in a large bowl. Add the eggs and crabmeat and gently fold to combine, adding more mayonnaise if the mixture seems dry. Season with salt and pepper.

2 // Mound the salad on each of the bread slices and garnish with the dill fronds.

HAM AND CHEDDAR PIE

WITH GREENS WITH APRICOT VINAIGRETTE

SERVES 4 TO 6

Take some help from your freezer section and use prepackaged puff pastry to make this golden-crusted, savory stuffed pie in no time. A thin layer of apricot jam adds a touch of sweetness that contrasts so nicely with salty ham and sharp cheddar; the flavor gets picked up in the dressing of a simple mixed green salad, too.

1 (17.3-ounce) package all-butter frozen puff pastry, defrosted but still cold

All-purpose flour, for rolling

1 large egg beaten with 2 tablespoons water

3 tablespoons whole-grain mustard

1 tablespoon apricot jam

½ pound thinly sliced country ham or Black Forest ham

6 ounces coarsely grated aged white cheddar cheese

Mixed Greens with Apricot Vinaigrette and Almonds (page 216)

1 // Preheat the oven to 400°F. Line a baking sheet with parchment paper.

2 // Unfold or unroll one sheet of the puff pastry on a lightly floured surface. Gently roll with a rolling pin to thin it out slightly. Put the pastry on the prepared baking sheet and brush the pastry from edge to edge with the egg wash. Combine the mustard and apricot jam in a small bowl and spread over the egg wash, leaving about a 1-inch border between the mustard and the edge of the pastry. Distribute the ham evenly over the mustard and then sprinkle the cheese over the ham.

3 // Roll out the second piece of puff pastry as before. Gently place it on top of the ham and cheese and press the edges together with your fingers. Gently fold about ½ inch of the edge over, creating a thick crust. Press the crust with the tines of a fork, dipping the fork in flour if the fork sticks to the puff pastry.

4 // Brush with the egg wash from edge to edge. Use a sharp knife to cut 3 vents through the top pastry. Bake the pie until puffed and golden brown, about 25 minutes. Remove to a rack and let cool for 10 minutes before serving. Serve the salad alongside.

BLACK PEPPER POPOVERS

FILLED WITH HERBED SCRAMBLED EGGS
AND GLAZED CANADIAN BACON

SERVES 6

The airy pockets of a popover are calling out to be filled with these creamy scrambled eggs, flecked with melted shreds of aged Vermont cheddar, bright green herbs, and lean and salty Canadian bacon, glazed with a sweet-tangy blend of warm maple syrup and sharp Dijon mustard.

¼ cup pure grade B maple syrup

1 heaping tablespoon Dijon mustard

6 slices Canadian bacon

12 large eggs

1 tablespoon finely chopped fresh parsley leaves

1 tablespoon finely chopped fresh chives

2 teaspoons finely chopped fresh tarragon

3 ounces grated aged white Vermont cheddar cheese

Kosher salt and freshly ground black pepper

6 tablespoons (¾ stick) unsalted butter, cut into pieces

Black Pepper Popovers (page 147)

1 // Preheat the oven to 425°F. Line a baking sheet with parchment.

2 // Whisk together the syrup and mustard in a small bowl. Put the bacon on the baking sheet and brush with some of the maple glaze. Bake the bacon, brushing with a little of the glaze a minute before removing from the oven, until lightly golden brown and crisp.

3 // Whisk together the eggs, herbs, and cheddar in a large bowl and season with salt and pepper. Heat the butter in a large nonstick pan over medium-low heat until it begins to sizzle. Add the eggs and slowly cook, stirring with a wooden spoon, until soft curds form.

4 // Open the popovers and fill each one with a slice of the bacon and top with some of the scrambled eggs.

COUNTRY HAM AND FRIED EGG

ON ANGEL BISCUITS

SERVES 4

This is classic southern fare. Split and filled with slivers of salty ham and a satisfying fried egg, these light and fluffy biscuits make a breakfast sandwich I would eat any time, any day.

4 tablespoons (½ stick) unsalted butter

4 large eggs

Kosher salt and freshly ground black pepper

¼ pound very thinly sliced country ham

4 Angel Biscuits (page 153), warm, split

1 // Heat the butter in a large nonstick sauté pan over medium-high heat until it begins to sizzle. Add the eggs, season with salt and pepper, and cook until the white is set. Gently flip over and continue to cook for another minute.

2 // Put a few slices of ham on the bottom of each biscuit and top with an egg. Top with the other half of the biscuit and serve immediately.

FRUIT DISHES & FRUIT SALADS

APRICOT AND RASPBERRY GRANOLA GRATIN

WITH RASPBERRY HONEY YOGURT

SERVES 4 TO 6

Apricots and raspberries are late summer favorites, each with a slightly tart note to balance its natural sweetness. This could be a dessert, but a topping of wholesome, crunchy granola and a drizzle of yogurt and honey definitely make this a brunch-time go-to.

4 tablespoons (½ stick) unsalted butter, melted, plus more for the baking dish

1 cup whole milk

4 large eggs

1 cup all-purpose flour

2 tablespoons granulated sugar

2 tablespoons light brown sugar

1 teaspoon pure vanilla extract

¼ teaspoon fine sea salt

8 ripe fresh apricots, halved, pitted, and cut into 8 pieces each

1 cup fresh raspberries

1 cup low-fat granola

½ cup sliced almonds

1 cup plain Greek nonfat yogurt

3 tablespoons honey, preferably raspberry honey

1 // Preheat the oven to 425°F. Brush a 9-inch gratin dish with butter.

2 // In a medium bowl, whisk together the milk and eggs. Whisk in the flour, both types of sugar, butter, vanilla, and salt until smooth. Pour the batter into the baking dish and arrange the apricot slices and raspberries on top of the batter.

3 // Bake for 20 minutes. Sprinkle the top with the granola and almonds and bake until the batter is light brown and set and the fruit is tender, 5 to 10 minutes more. Let cool for 20 minutes before serving.

4 // Mix together the yogurt and honey. Serve drizzled over the gratin.

YOGURT CRÈME BRÛLÉE
WITH FRESH FRUIT AND GRANOLA

SERVES 4

This dish combines the best of the decadent luxurious dessert with the classic healthful breakfast for a brunch treat that is light but also special—thanks to a golden brown crust of caramelized sugar. If you have a kitchen blowtorch, you've got to give this one a try.

16 ounces plain 2% Greek yogurt

1 teaspoon pure vanilla extract or ½ vanilla bean, split lengthwise, seeds scraped

1 pint fresh blueberries, raspberries, blackberries, or strawberries (or a combination)

Granulated sugar

2 teaspoons fresh lemon juice

½ cup granola

8 teaspoons turbinado sugar

1 // Mix together the yogurt and vanilla in a medium bowl until combined. Cover and refrigerate for at least 30 minutes to allow the flavors to meld.

2 // Put the berries in a small saucepan, add ¼ cup water, and simmer until just softened, about 5 minutes. Add granulated sugar to taste and stir in the lemon juice. Let cool slightly.

3 // Divide the fruit among four 8-ounce ramekins and top with the granola. Fill the ramekins to the top with the yogurt (discard the vanilla bean if using). Cover and put in the freezer for 5 minutes.

4 // Sprinkle 2 teaspoons of turbinado sugar over each ramekin. Caramelize the sugar with a blowtorch by slowly sweeping the flame back and forth. Let the sugar harden, about 2 minutes, before serving.

NOTE

This recipe simply will not work under the broiler; the yogurt will melt. A small blowtorch (found at specialty kitchen stores or online) is essential.

CHOCOLATE-ORANGE YOGURT PANNA COTTA
WITH CHOCOLATE-COCONUT GRANOLA

SERVES 8

Chocolate and panna cotta are words that generally signify a dish of sweet decadence. But factor in the yogurt and granola elements, top it all with a fresh salad of bright orange segments, and you have a dish you can feel good about! The granola, chunky and full of chopped almonds, is a great take-along, high-energy snack, in addition to being a welcome crunchy topping for the smooth panna cotta.

2 teaspoons unflavored powdered gelatin

2 cups low-fat (1%) milk

¾ cup sugar

3 ounces semisweet chocolate, finely chopped

¼ cup unsweetened cocoa powder

1⅔ cups plain nonfat Greek yogurt

1 teaspoon pure vanilla extract

2 teaspoons grated orange zest

Nonstick cooking spray

2 oranges, segmented (see page 54)

Chocolate-Coconut Granola (recipe opposite)

1 // In a small bowl, sprinkle the gelatin over ½ cup of the milk. Let stand for 1 minute, then stir, and let stand for about 10 more minutes to soften.

2 // In a medium saucepan, whisk the remaining 1½ cups milk, the sugar, chocolate, and cocoa over medium heat until the mixture begins to simmer, about 3 minutes. Add the gelatin mixture and whisk gently until it dissolves, 2 to 3 minutes. Let cool for 10 minutes.

3 // In a large bowl, whisk the yogurt with the vanilla until smooth. Pour the chocolate mixture through a fine-mesh strainer into the yogurt, add the orange zest, and then whisk to combine.

4 // Spray 8 ramekins (⅔-cup size) with cooking spray. Divide the yogurt mixture among the ramekins. Cover and refrigerate until set, at least 4½ hours and up to 2 days.

5 // Run a small metal spatula between the panna cotta and sides of each ramekin to loosen. Immerse the ramekins one at a time just below the rim in hot water until the edges of the dessert soften, 20 to 30 seconds; lift out and dry the bottom of the ramekins. Invert a small plate over each. Hold the plate and ramekin together and give a firm shake to release each panna cotta, easing it out gently with a spatula if needed.

6 // Top each panna cotta with orange segments and some of the granola and serve.

CHOCOLATE-COCONUT GRANOLA

MAKES ABOUT 4 CUPS

¼ cup plus 1 tablespoon coconut oil

¼ cup sugar

¼ cup clover honey

⅓ cup unsweetened cocoa powder

Pinch of fine sea salt

⅛ teaspoon pure coconut extract

⅛ teaspoon pure vanilla extract

2½ cups rolled oats

½ cup raw whole almonds, coarsely chopped

½ cup coconut chips, coarsely chopped

¼ cup best-quality white chocolate chips

¼ cup best-quality bittersweet chocolate chips

1 // Preheat the oven to 275°F. Brush a baking sheet with 1 tablespoon of the coconut oil.

2 // Heat the remaining ¼ cup oil over medium heat in a small saucepan. Whisk in the sugar, honey, cocoa powder, and salt and bring to a simmer. Cook, whisking constantly, until smooth and the sugar is completely melted. Stir in the coconut and vanilla extracts.

3 // Combine the oats, almonds, and coconut chips in a bowl. Add the warm cocoa mixture and mix with a rubber spatula until the oat mixture is completely coated. Transfer the mixture to the prepared baking sheet and press into an even layer. Bake until crisp, 50 minutes. Turn off the oven and let sit in the warm oven for 30 minutes longer. Remove to a rack and let cool.

4 // Break the granola into small pieces and stir in the white and dark chocolate chips. Store in an airtight container.

CITRUS BLUEBERRY SALAD

WITH ALMOND RELISH AND MINTED SUGAR

SERVES 8

This salad, with its rainbow array of yellow, orange, and pink citrus segments shot through with purple blueberries, is flat-out gorgeous. The citrus juices, cooked with sweetly spicy ginger and honey, become the base of a glossy dressing that enhances the fruit's sweet, acidic nature. The relish is a tasty mix of toasted almonds tossed with green-flecked minted sugar.

¼ cup sugar

8 fresh mint leaves, chopped

2 ruby red grapefruits, segmented (see page 54), juice reserved

2 yellow grapefruits, segmented (see page 54), juice reserved

2 navel oranges, segmented (see page 54), juice reserved

4 clementines, segmented (see page 54), juice reserved

Fresh orange or grapefruit juice, if needed

1 (2-inch) piece fresh ginger, cut in half

1 tablespoon honey

1 pint fresh blueberries

½ cup toasted almonds, chopped

1 // Put the sugar and mint in a food processor and process until smooth. Transfer to a small bowl.

2 // Combine the grapefruit, orange, and clementine segments in a large decorative bowl.

3 // Combine the reserved juices in a small saucepan (you should have at least 2 cups; if you don't, add enough fresh orange or grapefruit juice to make up the difference) with the ginger and bring to a boil over high heat. Boil until the mixture reduces by half. Stir in the honey and let cool to room temperature, at least 30 minutes.

4 // Remove the ginger, pour the mixture over the citrus, cover, and refrigerate for at least 1 hour and up to 24 hours.

5 // Just before serving, stir in the blueberries. Mix together the almonds and mint sugar and sprinkle over the top of the salad.

RASPBERRIES AND CREAM

SERVES 4 TO 6

**Sweet, tart, and refreshing, this berry granita is a
different approach to yogurt and fruit in the morning.
Use ripe berries at the peak of their season for best
results. This is perfect for a summer brunch at the
beach.**

1 pound ripe raspberries or blackberries

¼ cup plus 2 tablespoons sugar

2 tablespoons Chambord or, if using blackberries,
    Marie Brizard

2 teaspoons fresh lemon juice

½ cup heavy cream, very cold

½ vanilla bean, split lengthwise, seeds scraped

1½ cups French-style plain or vanilla yogurt

1 // Toss the berries with ¼ cup of the sugar and the
Chambord and let macerate at room temperature
until they have released their juices, 1½ hours.

2 // Pour the berry mixture into a blender, add
½ cup water and the lemon juice, and blend
until smooth. Strain through a fine-mesh sieve.
Discard the solids. Pour the liquid into a shallow
glass or plastic container that measures about
8 × 12 inches. Freeze until the edges are set, about
an hour.

3 // Remove the container from the freezer and,
using a fork, scrape any frozen parts of the mixture
from the edges into the center, breaking up any
large frozen pieces. Return the container to the
freezer and continue to scrape as before every
30 minutes, until you have nothing but flaky
crystals.

4 // Meanwhile, put a large stainless-steel bowl and
whisk in the freezer for 10 minutes. Remove and
add the cream, the remaining 2 tablespoons sugar,
and the vanilla seeds. Whip until soft peaks form.
Gently whisk in the yogurt, cover, and refrigerate
for at least 30 minutes and up to 2 hours.

5 // Spoon some of the yogurt cream into 4 or
6 parfait glasses, spoon the granita on top of the
cream, and drizzle the top with more of the cream.

STRAWBERRIES
FILLED WITH "CLOTTED" CREAM

SERVES 4 TO 6

This recipe is an easy, delicious approximation, made by blending whipped sweet cream with rich, silky mascarpone cheese. It's a delicious cheat, perfect for brunch—or afternoon tea.

1 cup mascarpone cheese

½ cup heavy cream, very cold

3 tablespoons confectioners' sugar

¼ teaspoon pure vanilla extract

1 vanilla bean, split lengthwise, seeds scraped

1 teaspoon grated orange zest

16 large fresh strawberries

1 // Combine the mascarpone, cream, sugar, vanilla, vanilla bean seeds, and orange zest in the bowl of a stand mixer and whip until soft peaks form. Scrape the mixture into a pastry bag fitted with a star tip.

2 // The strawberries need to stand flat. Cut the green leaves off the strawberries so they will stand upright when placed on the platter. With a small, sharp knife, cut an × in each strawberry, cutting almost to the bottom. Gently, with your fingertips, spread each strawberry apart to make 4 "petals."

3 // Fill each strawberry carefully with the cream and serve immediately.

TROPICAL FRUIT SALAD
WITH GINGER SYRUP

SERVES 6 TO 8

Sweet and spicy ginger combines with fragrant lime zest to add incredible flavor to a glossy simple syrup that lightly coats slices of exotic, colorful tropical fruits. This fresh, vibrant salad is a far cry from the canned fruit cocktail I knew as a child.

¼ cup sugar

1 (3-inch) piece fresh ginger, peeled and chopped

Grated zest of 1 lime

1 papaya, peeled, halved, seeded, and sliced

1 mango, peeled, halved, seeded, and sliced

4 kiwis, peeled, quartered, and sliced

½ small pineapple, cut into chunks

2 oranges, segmented (see page 54)

1 // Combine ¼ cup water and the sugar, ginger, and lime zest in a small saucepan, bring to a boil, and cook until the sugar is melted, about 1 minute. Remove from the heat, cover, and refrigerate until cold.

2 // Strain the syrup into a large bowl, add the fruit, and toss to coat. Cover and refrigerate until cold, at least 1 hour and up to 24 hours.

3 // Serve in small bowls.

GRAPEFRUIT SALAD
WITH HONEY-MINT DRESSING

SERVES 4

I love grapefruit and all of its refreshing astringency. Just a couple of ingredients and a few steps separate this salad from a simple half grapefruit in a bowl, but that sweet, mellowing honey and fresh, bright mint elevate pale white and deep pink segments of the citrus into an elegant, second-helping-worthy dish.

2 tablespoons clover honey

2 tablespoons finely chopped fresh mint

2 white grapefruits, segmented (see page 54), juice reserved

2 ruby red grapefruits, segmented (see page 54), juice reserved

Whisk the honey and mint into the grapefruit juice. Arrange the grapefruit segments on a platter or in a shallow bowl and drizzle with the dressing.

FROMAGE BLANC

WITH LAVENDER HONEY, STONE FRUIT, AND PINE NUTS

SERVES 4 TO 6

Sometimes the best recipes are those that aren't recipes at all, but rather simple pairings of ingredients that are each at the top of their game. This Provençal-inspired plating of fresh, creamy fromage blanc with delicately floral lavender honey, juicy ripe stone fruit, and buttery, crunchy pine nuts is the perfect example.

16 ounces fromage blanc

4 large ripe nectarines, peaches, or plums, halved, pitted, and sliced

¼ cup lavender honey

2 tablespoons toasted pine nuts

Put the fromage blanc in a shallow bowl, arrange the fruit around and on top, drizzle with the honey, and garnish with the pine nuts.

SAVORY
SIDE
DISHES

PEACH AND ARUGULA SALAD

WITH CRISPY PANCETTA AND GORGONZOLA

SERVES 4

This gorgeous sweet and savory salad is inspired by the Italian countryside. The blend of bitter arugula, ripe peaches, and salty pancetta—dressed with a sweetly acidic mix of lemon juice, balsamic vinegar, honey, and olive oil—is in perfect balance. A thin layer of sweet fig preserves enhances and balances the pungent Gorgonzola.

1 tablespoon canola oil

1 (½-inch-thick) slice pancetta, diced

2 tablespoons fresh lemon juice

1 tablespoon balsamic vinegar

2 teaspoons clover honey

Kosher salt and freshly ground black pepper

¼ cup extra-virgin olive oil

2 ounces baby arugula

2 ripe peaches, halved and pitted

½ cup crumbled Gorgonzola

Toasted sliced ciabatta

Fig preserves

1 // Heat the canola oil in a medium sauté pan over medium heat. Add the pancetta and cook until golden brown and crisp, 8 minutes. Remove the pancetta with a slotted spoon to a plate lined with paper towels.

2 // Whisk together the lemon juice, vinegar, and honey in a large bowl and season with salt and pepper. Whisk in the extra-virgin olive oil, add the arugula, and toss to combine.

3 // Transfer the greens to a platter, top with the peach halves, and sprinkle with the Gorgonzola and pancetta. Serve with toast and fig preserves on the side.

ARUGULA

WITH TOMATO VINAIGRETTE

SERVES 2

I am a big proponent of serving rich dishes, such as Hang Town Fry (page 119), with a bright and acidic vinaigrette to counterbalance any heaviness. This tomato vinaigrette, packed with flavorful sharp Dijon mustard, lemony parsley, and pungent garlic, does the trick. I especially like it as a dressing for peppery arugula, but it would work well with other greens, too.

1 large plum tomato, seeded and chopped

3 tablespoons red wine vinegar

1 teaspoon Dijon mustard

1 garlic clove

1 tablespoon fresh flat-leaf parsley

Kosher salt and freshly ground black pepper

6 tablespoons extra-virgin olive oil

2 ounces arugula

Combine the tomato, vinegar, mustard, garlic, parsley, and salt and pepper to taste in a blender and blend until smooth. With the motor running, slowly add the oil and blend until emulsified. Put the arugula in a bowl and lightly dress with some of the dressing.

MIXED GREENS

WITH APRICOT VINAIGRETTE AND ALMONDS

SERVES 4 TO 6

Adding a touch of fruit preserves is a great way to add sweetness and body to your basic vinaigrette. If you aren't a fan of apricots, orange marmalade would be an excellent substitute.

3 tablespoons Champagne vinegar

1 heaping tablespoon apricot jam

Kosher salt and freshly ground black pepper

¼ cup extra-virgin olive oil

3 ounces mixed baby greens

¼ cup lightly toasted sliced almonds

Whisk together the vinegar and jam in a small bowl and season with salt and pepper. Slowly whisk in the oil until emulsified. Put the greens in a large bowl, toss with the vinaigrette, and top with the nuts.

BRUSSELS SPROUT–APPLE SALAD

WITH MAPLE-THYME VINAIGRETTE

SERVES 4

This fall-to-winter salad is delicious on its own or as a side dish, and can also be used as a bed for a simply prepared protein, such as seared salmon, and served as a main course. You may be more familiar with them roasted, but when very thinly sliced, Brussels sprouts transform into a delicate, gorgeous pale green slaw.

5 tablespoons apple cider vinegar

2 tablespoons pure grade B maple syrup

2 teaspoons Dijon mustard

1 teaspoon finely chopped fresh thyme

Kosher salt and freshly ground black pepper

½ cup extra-virgin olive oil

10 ounces Brussels sprouts, trimmed and halved

1 large Gala apple, halved and cored

2 teaspoons fresh lemon juice

½ small red onion, thinly sliced

¼ cup dried cranberries

1 // Whisk together the vinegar, maple syrup, mustard, and thyme in a small bowl. Season with salt and pepper and then slowly whisk in the oil until emulsified.

2 // Fit the food processor with the slicing disk and slice all the Brussels sprouts. Remove to a large bowl. Fluff and separate the slices with your fingers.

3 // Fit the food processor with the shredding disk and grate the apple. Add the apple to the Brussels sprouts and sprinkle with the lemon juice and some of the vinaigrette. Add the onion and cranberries, drizzle with more of the vinaigrette, and season with salt and pepper. Toss to combine and transfer to a platter.

TOMATO STRATA

SERVES 4 TO 6

More of a baked panzanella than anything else, this strata, bursting with tomato flavor, is a lovely side dish for poached or scrambled eggs. It can be prepared in advance and is delicious served hot or at room temperature.

½ cup plus 2 tablespoons olive oil, plus more
for the dish

3 garlic cloves, smashed

1 medium French baguette, cut into ½-inch dice

Kosher salt and freshly ground black pepper

3 pounds ripe beefsteak tomatoes, seeded and diced

Pinch of sugar

Pinch of red pepper flakes

6 large eggs

¼ cup lightly packed thinly sliced basil leaves

1 cup freshly grated Romano cheese

1 // Preheat the oven to 350°F. Grease a 2-quart baking dish with olive oil.

2 // Put ½ cup of the oil and the garlic cloves in a large high-sided sauté pan over medium heat and cook the garlic until lightly golden brown on both sides, about 2 minutes. Add the bread cubes and salt and pepper and cook, stirring occasionally, until the bread cubes are lightly golden brown on all sides, 5 minutes. Add the tomatoes, sugar, and red pepper flakes to the pan and continue to cook, stirring often, for 5 minutes. Remove from the heat, transfer to a bowl, and let cool.

3 // Whisk the eggs in a small bowl and add to the tomato mixture. Season with salt and pepper and add the basil. Pour into the prepared baking dish. Sprinkle evenly with the cheese and drizzle with the remaining 2 tablespoons olive oil. Bake until the top is browned and the tomatoes are bubbly, about 30 minutes.

ROASTED TOMATOES
WITH HERB BREAD CRUMBS

SERVES 4 TO 6

This simple, savory side dish goes as well with a plate of eggs at brunch as it would with a piece of grilled chicken at dinner. Oven roasting is a great way to coax amazing amounts of flavor out of lackluster tomatoes, whichever side of ripe they may fall. Garlicky, toasty bread crumbs loaded with parsley add a bit of crunch to contrast with the soft tomatoes.

6 plum tomatoes, halved lengthwise

Unsalted butter, for the baking dish

5 tablespoons olive oil

Kosher salt and freshly ground black pepper

1 garlic clove, finely chopped

1 cup fresh bread crumbs

2 tablespoons finely chopped fresh flat-leaf parsley

1 // Preheat the oven to 400°F.

2 // Put the tomato halves in a lightly buttered baking dish, cut side up, drizzle with 2 tablespoons of the olive oil, and season with salt and pepper. Bake for 10 minutes.

3 // Meanwhile, heat the remaining 3 tablespoons oil in a medium sauté pan over medium heat. Add the garlic and cook for 30 seconds. Add the bread crumbs and season with salt and pepper. Cook the crumbs, stirring constantly, until light golden brown. Remove from the heat and stir in the parsley.

4 // Remove the tomatoes from the oven and top each with about 1 tablespoon of the crumbs. Return to the oven and continue baking until the tomatoes are soft and the crumbs become golden brown and crisp, about 15 minutes longer. Serve hot or at room temperature.

WILD MUSHROOM— YUKON GOLD HASH

SERVES 4

Earthy wild mushrooms, loaded with shallot, thyme, and parsley, add a rich and meaty element to this hash. I parboil Yukon gold potatoes, which have a gorgeous yellow flesh and buttery taste, before dicing and then sautéing them until golden brown and crisp. These potatoes are a wonderful side dish for any savory brunch dish and the perfect base for simply poached eggs.

½ ounce dried porcini mushrooms

2 pounds Yukon gold potatoes

Kosher salt and freshly ground black pepper

4 tablespoons (½ stick) unsalted butter

4 tablespoons canola oil

1½ pounds "wild" fresh mushrooms, such as chanterelle, cremini, or oyster, roughly chopped

1 large shallot, finely diced

Splash of aged sherry vinegar

1 tablespoon finely chopped fresh thyme leaves

¼ cup chopped fresh flat-leaf parsley

1 // Bring 1 cup water to a boil. Put the porcini mushrooms in a small bowl, add the boiling water, and let sit until soft, about 30 minutes.

2 // Meanwhile, put the potatoes in a large pot, cover with cold water by 2 inches, and add 2 tablespoons salt. Bring to a boil over high heat and cook until a skewer inserted into the center of each potato meets no resistance, about 20 minutes. Drain well and let cool slightly while you prepare the mushrooms.

3 // Heat 2 tablespoons of the butter and 2 tablespoons of the canola oil in a large sauté pan over high heat until the mixture begins to shimmer. Add the fresh mushrooms and shallot and cook until the mushrooms are golden brown, all of their liquid has evaporated, and the shallot is tender, about 15 minutes.

4 // Remove the porcini mushrooms from their soaking liquid, coarsely chop, and add to the pan. Strain the soaking liquid into the mushrooms, taking care not to add any sediment at the bottom, and simmer until evaporated. Stir in the vinegar, thyme, parsley, and salt and pepper to taste. Remove from the heat.

5 // Dice the potatoes into ½-inch pieces, leaving the skin on. Heat the remaining 2 tablespoons butter and remaining 2 tablespoons oil in a large nonstick sauté pan over high heat until the mixture begins to shimmer. Add the potatoes, season with salt and pepper, and cook until lightly golden brown on all sides, about 10 minutes.

6 // Add the mushrooms to the potatoes and cook to warm through. Transfer to a platter and serve hot or at room temperature.

CAST-IRON HOME FRIES
WITH ROASTED GREEN CHILES AND
CREAMY GARLIC DRESSING

SERVES 4 TO 6

This dish is one part home fries, one part salad, and all parts delicious. Cubes of fluffy russet potato are cooked until golden brown and crisp in a cast-iron pan, then tossed together with vibrant cilantro, assertively oniony green onions, peppery strips of roasted poblanos, and slightly bitter ribbons of deep purple radicchio. A creamy mayonnaise-based garlic dressing, bright with sharp Dijon mustard, binds each element together.

3 large russet potatoes (3 pounds), scrubbed

Kosher salt and freshly ground black pepper

3 tablespoons canola oil, plus more if needed

2 poblano chiles, roasted (see page 136), peeled, seeded, and thinly sliced

1 small head radicchio, halved and thinly sliced

Creamy Garlic Dressing (recipe follows)

¼ cup fresh cilantro leaves, chopped

3 green onions, green and pale green parts, thinly sliced

1 // Put the potatoes in a large saucepan and add enough cold water to cover by 2 inches. Add 2 tablespoons salt to the water, bring to a boil over high heat, and boil until a skewer or paring knife inserted into the center meets with no resistance, about 25 minutes, depending on the size of the potatoes. Drain the potatoes and let cool for at least 5 minutes on a cutting board. Cut each potato into 1-inch dice.

2 // Heat the oil in a large cast-iron skillet over high heat until the oil begins to shimmer. Add the potatoes in a single layer and cook until a crust has formed on the bottom, about 5 minutes. Gently turn them and cook until all sides are golden brown and crisp, adding more oil if needed, about 5 minutes more.

3 // Transfer the potatoes to a bowl, add the chiles, radicchio, and dressing and gently stir to combine. Fold in the cilantro and green onions and season with salt and pepper. Serve warm or at room temperature.

CREAMY GARLIC DRESSING
MAKES ABOUT ½ CUP

½ cup mayonnaise

2 tablespoons white wine vinegar

1 heaping tablespoon Dijon mustard

3 garlic cloves, smashed and chopped to a paste

Kosher salt and freshly ground black pepper

Whisk together the mayonnaise, vinegar, mustard, and garlic in a bowl and season with salt and pepper. Let sit for 30 minutes to allow the flavors to meld before serving.

POTATO PANCAKES
WITH CHUNKY APPLESAUCE AND
CINNAMON CRÈME FRAÎCHE

A tasty Eastern European treat, these savory potato pancakes are traditionally served with either applesauce or sour cream, but I can never choose one over the other. I sub a smooth, sweetly cinnamon-scented crème fraîche for the usual plain sour cream. The shredded onion is key in making sure the crisp potato cakes have lots of flavor.

1 cup crème fraîche

1 teaspoon ground cinnamon

1 large russet potato (1 pound), peeled

1 small onion, peeled

¼ cup all-purpose flour

Pinch of baking powder

1 large egg, lightly beaten

1 teaspoon kosher salt

¼ teaspoon freshly ground pepper

Canola oil

Chunky Granny Smith Applesauce (page 56)

1 // Whisk together the crème fraîche and cinnamon, cover, and refrigerate for at least 30 minutes or until serving to allow the flavors to meld.

2 // On the large holes of a box grater, coarsely shred the potato and onion. Transfer to a colander and squeeze as dry as possible. Let stand for 2 minutes and then squeeze dry again. Put the potato mixture in a large bowl, add the flour, baking powder, egg, salt, and pepper and gently fold to combine.

3 // In a large cast-iron skillet, heat 2 tablespoons canola oil until shimmering. Drop heaping tablespoons of the potato mixture into the skillet and flatten them with the back of the spoon. Cook the pancakes over moderately high heat until the edges are golden, 1½ to 2 minutes, flip, and cook until golden on the bottom, about 1 minute. Drain on paper towels. Repeat with the remaining potato mixture, adding more oil to the skillet as needed.

4 // Serve the hot potato pancakes topped with the applesauce and a small dollop of cinnamon crème fraîche.

NOTE

You can make the potato pancakes in advance and then reheat them in a single layer on a baking sheet in a 400°F oven until they're crisp again. BONUS: If you undercooked them a bit or didn't get the browning on them you'd hoped for, you can compensate for this in the oven.

SPICY HOME FRIES

SERVES 4 TO 6

Highly seasoned with just enough heat to cut through a foggy morning, these spicy home fries are the ideal accompaniment to a south-of-the-border-inspired brunch, such as ranch-style eggs. That said, they have enough flavor to stand on their own when topped with a sunny-side-up egg. Don't mess with the potatoes too much as they cook; let that golden crust develop for a deliciously crisp bottom edge.

4 large russet potatoes (4 pounds), peeled and cut into 1-inch dice

Kosher salt and freshly ground black pepper

¼ cup canola oil

4 tablespoons (½ stick) unsalted butter

1 medium Spanish onion, finely diced

1 jalapeño, finely diced

3 garlic cloves, finely chopped

2 tablespoons ancho chile powder

Pinch of cayenne pepper

½ cup chopped fresh cilantro

1 // Put the potatoes in a large saucepan, cover with cold water, and add 1 tablespoon salt. Bring to a boil over high heat and cook until the potatoes fall apart when a fork is inserted, 20 to 25 minutes. Drain well.

2 // Heat the oil and butter over medium heat in a large sauté pan. Add the onion and jalapeño and cook until soft, about 5 minutes. Add the garlic and cook for 30 seconds. Stir in the ancho chile powder and cayenne.

3 // Add the potatoes, season with salt and pepper, and mix, slightly mashing the potatoes with a metal spatula. Press into an even layer and cook until golden brown on the bottom, 6 minutes. Turn over and gently mash again into an even layer and cook until the bottom is golden brown, 6 minutes. Stir in the cilantro and serve.

ROSEMARY HOME FRIES

WITH PANCETTA, PARMESAN, AND PARSLEY

SERVES 4 TO 6

A super fragrant, extra flavorful garlic- and rosemary-infused oil provides the background for crisp browned home fries punctuated with salty, chewy bites of pancetta. A sprinkle of nutty Parmesan and lots of bright, fresh parsley complete this awesome brunch side dish.

4 large russet potatoes (4 pounds)

Kosher salt and freshly ground black pepper

¼ cup canola oil, plus more if needed

2 tablespoons fresh rosemary leaves

2 garlic cloves, thinly sliced

1 (1-inch-thick) slice pancetta, diced

Pinch of red pepper flakes

Freshly grated Parmesan cheese

¼ cup chopped fresh flat-leaf parsley

1 // Put the potatoes in a pot and add enough water to cover by 2 inches. Season the water with salt, bring to a boil over high heat, and cook the potatoes until a skewer inserted into the center of each meets with just a little resistance, 20 to 25 minutes. Drain well, let cool slightly, and then cut into 1-inch dice.

2 // Meanwhile, combine the oil and rosemary in a blender, season with salt and pepper, and blend for 1 minute. Let the oil sit for 30 minutes before straining through a fine-mesh strainer into a small bowl.

3 // Heat the rosemary oil in a large cast-iron skillet over medium heat. Add the garlic and cook until lightly golden brown, 2 minutes. Remove with a slotted spoon to a plate lined with paper towels.

4 // Add the pancetta to the pan and cook until golden brown and crisp, about 5 minutes. Remove with a slotted spoon to the plate with the garlic.

5 // Add more oil to the pan, if none remains. Add the potatoes, season with salt and pepper, and cook until golden brown and crusty on all sides, about 7 minutes. Stir in the red pepper flakes, cheese, and parsley; transfer to a platter; and top with the garlic slices and pancetta.

YUCCA HASH BROWNS

WITH BACON, ONION, AND LIME-CILANTRO MOJO

A South American staple, yucca, or cassava, is a tuberous root with a bark-like exterior covering a smooth, bright white, hard, and dense interior. Super starchy with a slight sweetness, it cooks up much like a potato. The mojo, a garlicky citrus sauce loved throughout the Caribbean and Latin America, adds a punch of flavor, as does smoky, salty bacon.

2 pounds yucca, peeled and cut into ¾-inch dice

4 garlic cloves

1 bay leaf, preferably fresh

Kosher salt and freshly ground black pepper

12 ounces slab bacon, diced

2 tablespoons canola oil

1 small Spanish onion, diced

2 teaspoons ground cumin

Lime-Cilantro Mojo (recipe follows)

1 // Put the yucca, garlic, and bay leaf in a large saucepan, add enough cold water to cover by 2 inches, and season with salt and pepper. Bring to a boil over high heat, reduce the heat so the water simmers, and cook until the yucca is just tender, but not falling apart, 15 minutes. Drain well in a colander and then transfer to baking sheets lined with paper towels to drain again. Discard the garlic and bay leaf.

2 // Heat a large nonstick sauté pan over medium heat. Add the bacon and cook until the fat is rendered and the bacon is crisp. Remove with a slotted spoon and drain on a plate lined with paper towels.

3 // Increase the heat to high underneath the pan, add the oil to the bacon fat, and heat until it begins to shimmer. Add the onion and cumin and cook until soft, about 4 minutes. Add the yucca, season with salt and pepper, and cook until lightly golden brown on all sides, about 8 minutes.

4 // Transfer to a platter and drizzle with the lime-cilantro mojo.

LIME-CILANTRO MOJO
MAKES ABOUT ½ CUP

¼ cup fresh lime juice

2 tablespoons aged sherry vinegar

2 garlic cloves, finely chopped

½ jalapeño, finely diced

1 teaspoon clover honey

2 tablespoons finely chopped fresh cilantro leaves

Kosher salt and freshly ground black pepper

Stir together all of the ingredients in a small bowl and let sit at room temperature for at least 30 minutes to allow the flavors to meld.

SWEET POTATO HASH
WITH COUNTRY HAM

SERVES 4

Could anything be more southern than sweet potatoes and ham? Sweet potatoes are one of my favorite vegetables, and I use them in everything from tamales to gratins. Paired with salty ham, this hash is perfect topped with a fried egg or served as a side dish alongside of pancakes and waffles.

3 medium sweet potatoes, peeled

Kosher salt and freshly ground black pepper

1 (½-inch-thick) slice country ham

3 green onions, thinly sliced

¼ cup coarsely chopped fresh cilantro

1 tablespoon pureed canned chipotle in adobo

1 tablespoon honey

2 tablespoons canola oil

1 // In a medium saucepan, cover the sweet potatoes with cold water, season with salt, and bring to a boil over high heat. Reduce the heat and simmer until the potatoes are tender, 25 to 30 minutes. Drain the potatoes, then cut into ½-inch cubes.

2 // Cut the ham into small dice. Cook the ham in a large sauté pan over medium-high heat until golden brown all over, 5 minutes. Remove to a large bowl and mix in the sweet potatoes, green onions, cilantro, chipotle, and honey; season with salt and pepper. Form into 4 equal-sized patties.

3 // Heat the oil in a large sauté pan over high heat until just smoking. Season the patties with salt and pepper on both sides and cook until golden brown, about 2 minutes per side.

PATATAS BRAVAS HOME FRIES

WITH ROASTED TOMATO AIOLI

SERVES 4 TO 6

This is one of Spain's signature dishes; you can't hit a tapas bar without getting a plate of these cubed and fried potatoes, served with a side of spicy, rich, garlicky aioli. They are essentially home fries and are perfect for brunch.

3 large russet potatoes (3 pounds)

Kosher salt and freshly ground black pepper

Olive oil

½ small red onion, finely diced

2 garlic cloves, finely chopped

1 tablespoon smoked Spanish paprika

¾ cup mayonnaise

1 large plum tomato, halved, seeded, and roasted until soft

A few dashes of Tabasco sauce

Splash of aged sherry vinegar

Fresh flat-leaf parsley leaves

1 // Put the potatoes in a large saucepan and add enough cold water to cover by 2 inches. Add 2 tablespoons salt to the water, bring to a boil over high heat, and boil until a skewer or paring knife inserted into the center meets with no resistance, about 25 minutes, depending on the size of the potatoes. Drain the potatoes and let cool for at least 5 minutes on a cutting board. Peel and then cut each potato into 1-inch dice.

2 // Preheat the oven to 375°F. Put a baking sheet in the oven as it heats.

3 // Heat 1 tablespoon olive oil in a small sauté pan over medium heat. Add the onion and garlic and cook until soft, about 5 minutes. Add the paprika and cook for 30 seconds. Set aside to cool slightly.

4 // Combine the onion mixture, mayonnaise, tomato, Tabasco, and vinegar in a food processor and process until smooth; season with salt and pepper. Scrape into a bowl, cover, and refrigerate the roasted tomato aioli for at least 30 minutes and up to 24 hours to allow the flavors to meld.

5 // Heat 2 inches of oil in a large high-sided skillet over high heat until it begins to shimmer. Add the potatoes, season with salt and pepper, and cook until golden brown on all sides, about 7 minutes. Remove to a plate lined with paper towels to drain.

6 // Remove the hot baking sheet from the oven, put the potatoes on the sheet in an even layer, and bake until crisp, about 10 minutes. Season the potatoes with a bit more salt and transfer to a platter. Drizzle with some of the aioli and garnish with the parsley leaves. Serve hot with the remaining aioli on the side.

CHORIZO-POTATO CAKES
WITH BLACK BEANS AND SALSA VERDE

Amazing when paired with your favorite Mexican egg recipe, I could very happily eat this side dish as a main course! Potato pancakes, chock-full of garlicky, spicy chorizo sausage, are hearty on their own, and even more filling when topped with a spoonful of lightly spiced black beans. Citrusy salsa verde provides just the right fresh note to balance the smoky dish.

1½ pounds Yukon gold potatoes, peeled and cut into 1-inch dice

Kosher salt and freshly ground black pepper

Canola oil

6 ounces Mexican chorizo, homemade (page 247) or store-bought

1 large egg, lightly whisked

½ cup grated Monterey Jack cheese

¼ cup grated cotija cheese

3 tablespoons all-purpose flour, or more if needed

1½ cups panko bread crumbs

1 (15.5-ounce) can black beans, rinsed and drained

Pinch of ground cumin

Pinch of ground coriander

Salsa Verde (recipe opposite)

Thinly sliced green onion

1 // Put the potatoes in a medium saucepan and add cold water to cover by 2 inches along with 1 tablespoon kosher salt. Bring to a boil over high heat and cook until the potatoes are tender when pierced with a skewer, about 25 minutes. Drain well and return to the warm pan to dry, about 2 minutes. Mash the potatoes with a potato masher.

2 // Heat 1 tablespoon oil in a medium sauté pan over high heat. Add the chorizo and cook, stirring occasionally, until browned and in small pieces, about 10 minutes. Remove with a slotted spoon to a plate lined with paper towels.

3 // Put the mashed potatoes in a medium bowl and add the sausage, egg, both cheeses, and 3 tablespoons flour. Stir gently until combined; season with salt and pepper. If the mixture is too wet to form into a cake, stir in a little more flour. Cover and refrigerate until the mixture is firm and the flavors meld, at least 1 hour and up to 24 hours.

4 // Preheat the oven to 325°F.

5 // Spread the panko on a plate and season with salt and pepper. Using a ¼-cup measure, form the mixture into 2-inch cakes. Dredge each cake in the panko.

6 // Combine the beans, ½ cup cold water, the cumin, and the coriander in a small saucepan, bring to a simmer over medium heat, and cook until heated through.

7 // Meanwhile, heat ½ cup oil in a large nonstick sauté pan over medium-high heat until it begins to shimmer. Working in batches, fry the cakes on both sides until golden brown, about 2 minutes per side. Put the cakes in the oven to keep warm, if needed.

8 // Arrange the cakes on a platter, top with the salsa verde and black beans, and garnish with green onion.

SALSA VERDE
SERVES 4 TO 6

4 large tomatillos, husked, rinsed well, and finely diced

3 tablespoons finely diced red onion

Juice of 2 limes

2 tablespoons extra-virgin olive oil

Honey

Kosher salt and freshly ground black pepper

¼ cup chopped fresh cilantro

Combine the tomatillo, onion, lime juice, and oil in a medium bowl and season with honey and salt and pepper to taste. Fold in the cilantro.

EVERYTHING HASH BROWN CAKE

WITH GREEN ONION CRÈME FRAÎCHE

SERVES 4 TO 6

This is everything you love about an everything bagel—nutty sesame seeds, crunchy poppy seeds, toasty garlic, and just the right hit of salt—incorporated into a crisp hash brown cake. Green onion crème fraîche is a sophisticated take on scallion cream cheese, and bright pink pickled red onion adds far more flavor and freshness than burnt, dehydrated onion flakes ever could.

½ cup crème fraîche

2 green onions, dark green and pale green parts, thinly sliced

Kosher salt and freshly ground black pepper

½ cup clarified butter (page 95)

1 garlic clove, smashed

3 large russet potatoes (3 pounds), peeled

¾ teaspoon sesame seeds

¾ teaspoon poppy seeds

Pickled Red Onion (page 243)

Fresh flat-leaf parsley leaves

1 // Mix together the crème fraîche and green onion in a small bowl, season with salt and pepper, cover, and refrigerate until ready to serve.

2 // Heat ¼ cup of the clarified butter in a 12-inch seasoned cast-iron pan or nonstick skillet over medium-low heat, add the garlic clove, and cook until it is lightly golden brown on both sides and infuses the oil with the flavor of garlic, 5 minutes. Discard the garlic.

3 // Meanwhile, grate the potatoes using the large holes on a box grater. Toss the potatoes with the sesame and poppy seeds and season with salt and pepper. Add to the pan and stir to coat the potatoes with the butter. Using a spatula, gently press the potatoes into an even layer and then cook, shaking the skillet occasionally, until the edges are golden and crisp, about 10 minutes.

4 // Invert a large plate over the skillet and invert the skillet with the plate, so the potato cake falls onto the plate. Slide the potato cake, browned side up, back into the skillet. Pour the remaining ¼ cup butter around the edges of the potato cake and continue cooking until the potatoes are crisp on the bottom, about 10 minutes.

5 // Transfer to a cutting board and let cool for a few minutes. Spread the crème fraîche on top, scatter with the pickled onion, and garnish with the parsley leaves. Cut into wedges and serve.

FRIED GREEN TOMATOES

WITH SHRIMP RÉMOULADE

SERVES 4

I can think of few better things to do with a pile of unripened tomatoes than make this classic New Orleans delicacy. It just works—the tangy, crisp-coated green tomatoes, layered with sweet shrimp, and topped with a paprika-spiced, creamy, herbed rémoulade. Though often made with poached and chilled shrimp, this dish is improved, I think, when you sauté the shellfish instead.

8 (½-inch-thick) slices green tomato (about 3 tomatoes)

Kosher salt and freshly ground black pepper

2 cups coarsely ground yellow cornmeal

Canola oil

24 medium (31 to 40 size) shrimp, peeled and deveined

1 teaspoon finely chopped fresh thyme

4 cups shredded iceberg lettuce

1 cup Rémoulade Sauce (page 237)

Fresh flat-leaf parsley leaves

Smoked sweet Spanish paprika

1 // Preheat the oven to 300°F.

2 // Put the tomato slices on a baking sheet lined with paper towels and pat dry to remove some of the excess water. Season both sides with salt and pepper.

3 // Put the cornmeal in a large shallow bowl and season with salt and pepper. Dredge the tomatoes in the cornmeal on both sides and tap off the excess cornmeal.

4 // Heat ½ cup oil in a large sauté pan over medium-high heat until it begins to shimmer. Line a baking sheet with fresh paper towels. Working in batches of 4, fry the tomatoes until golden brown on both sides and just cooked through, about 1½ minutes per side. Remove with a slotted spatula to the baking sheet and season with salt. Once all of the tomatoes have been fried, transfer the baking sheet to the oven to keep them warm while you cook the shrimp.

5 // Heat 2 tablespoons oil in a large sauté pan over high heat until it begins to shimmer. Add the shrimp, season with salt and pepper, and cook, turning once, until lightly golden brown and just cooked through, about 3 minutes. Add the thyme and remove from the heat.

6 // Toss the lettuce with ½ cup of the rémoulade. Divide the lettuce over the tomatoes, top each with 3 shrimp, and drizzle with more of the dressing. Garnish with the parsley leaves and a sprinkling of smoked paprika.

RÉMOULADE SAUCE
MAKES ABOUT 2 CUPS

Grated zest and juice of 1 lemon

1 large egg

¼ cup Creole mustard

2 tablespoons prepared horseradish

½ teaspoon kosher salt

¼ teaspoon freshly ground black pepper

½ teaspoon smoked sweet Spanish paprika

1 cup canola oil

3 tablespoons ketchup

3 tablespoons white wine vinegar

2 garlic cloves, smashed and chopped to a paste

2 tablespoons finely chopped fresh flat-leaf parsley

¼ cup finely diced celery

¼ cup finely diced red onion

2 teaspoons Worcestershire sauce

2 or 3 dashes Tabasco sauce, to taste

Whisk together the lemon zest and juice, egg, mustard, horseradish, salt, pepper, and paprika in a medium bowl. Gradually add the oil in a slow, steady stream, whisking constantly, until the oil is incorporated and the mixture is emulsified. Whisk in the ketchup, vinegar, garlic, parsley, celery, onion, Worcestershire, and Tabasco. Cover with plastic wrap and refrigerate for at least 1 hour and up to 24 hours to allow the flavors to meld. Leftovers will keep, refrigerated, for up to a couple of days.

CHEESY CORN AND SWEET ONION GRITS

SERVES 4 TO 6

Good grits are such a comforting, soul-warming dish. Studded with sweet kernels of fresh corn and even sweeter Vidalia onion, these grits get a nice balancing shot of salty flavor and richness from a combination of sharp Romano and aged cheddar cheeses. They make any morning better.

2 tablespoons unsalted butter

1 tablespoon canola oil

1 small Vidalia onion, finely diced

3 ears fresh corn, kernels removed from the cobs

Kosher salt and freshly ground black pepper

2 cups whole milk

1½ cups stone-ground grits

1½ cups grated aged white cheddar cheese

¼ cup freshly grated Romano cheese

3 green onions, green and pale green parts, thinly sliced

1 // Heat the butter and oil in a large saucepan over medium-high heat. Add the onion and cook until soft, about 4 minutes. Add the corn, season with salt and pepper, and cook for a few minutes. Add the milk and 3 cups water and bring to a boil.

2 // Slowly whisk in the grits until combined and continue whisking until smooth. Reduce the heat to low and continue cooking, stirring occasionally, until thickened and smooth, about 30 minutes, adding more water if needed to keep the mixture creamy.

3 // Remove from the heat and whisk in the cheeses and green onions. Serve hot.

JOHNNY GRIDDLE CAKES

Johnnycakes are one of this country's earliest recipes, thanks to the Pawtucket Indians of Rhode Island. I lighten them a bit by separating the eggs and beating the whites until fluffy. Once you've tried these, you'll understand why we're still making these tasty sweetened cornmeal pancakes today.

1 cup all-purpose flour

½ cup plus 1 tablespoon fine yellow or white cornmeal

2 tablespoons sugar

1 tablespoon baking powder

2 teaspoons kosher salt

¾ cup whole milk

2 teaspoons clover honey

2 large egg yolks

2 large egg whites

6 tablespoons (¾ stick) unsalted butter, melted and cooled

1 // Preheat the oven to 300°F.

2 // Whisk together the flour, cornmeal, sugar, baking powder, and salt in a medium bowl. Whisk together the milk, honey, and egg yolks in another medium bowl. With a clean whisk, whip the egg whites in a third medium bowl until stiff peaks form.

3 // Add the milk mixture to the flour mixture and stir until just combined. Gently fold in the egg whites and then stir in 2 tablespoons of the melted butter. Let the batter rest for 10 minutes.

4 // Heat a large nonstick sauté pan, cast-iron pan, or griddle over medium-high heat. Brush the pan with some of the remaining melted butter.

5 // Working in batches, spoon scant ¼ cupfuls of the batter onto the pan. Spread the batter slightly using a small offset spatula or the back of a spoon just to even out the top of each cake. Cook until light golden brown on each side, about 1 minute 30 seconds per side. Transfer to a baking sheet and keep warm in the oven and repeat with the remaining butter and batter. Serve hot.

GREEN RICE

SERVES 4 TO 6

This luxuriously rich and creamy rice dish has spent some time on the menu at Mesa Grill, where it is always a customer (and chef) favorite. A dynamic, flavorful mixture of fragrant cilantro, sharp green onions, and deep peppery poblano chiles provides the dish's namesake green color.

1½ cups heavy cream

1½ cups long-grain white rice

Kosher salt and freshly ground black pepper

2 poblano chiles, roasted (see page 136), peeled, seeded, and finely diced

3 green onions, thinly sliced

¼ cup finely chopped fresh cilantro

1 // Pour the cream into a small saucepan and bring to a boil over high heat. Lower the heat to medium and simmer until reduced by half.

2 // Meanwhile, bring 2¾ cups water to a boil in a medium saucepan over high heat. Stir in the rice and season with salt. Bring to a boil again, stir, and top the pan with a lid. Reduce the heat to medium and simmer until all of the liquid is absorbed, 15 to 18 minutes.

3 // Remove the rice from the heat and let sit for 5 minutes with the lid on. Remove the lid and fluff with a fork. Return the rice to the stove over medium heat, add the reduced cream, and season with salt and pepper. Stir in the poblanos, green onions, and cilantro. Serve hot.

HOMEMADE WHITEFISH SALAD

SERVES 4 TO 6

One of the luxuries of being a New Yorker is knowing that a great deli and a delicious breakfast of a bagel with whitefish salad is always just a few blocks away. Salty, creamy, and wonderfully smoky, whitefish salad is just a couple of steps but a world of flavor beyond canned tuna salad.

¾ cup mayonnaise

½ teaspoon grated lemon zest

2 tablespoons fresh lemon juice

½ small red onion, finely diced

1 large stalk celery, finely diced

2 pounds smoked whitefish, skinned, boned, and flaked

Kosher salt and freshly ground black pepper

Pickled Red Onion (recipe follows)

Whisk together the mayonnaise, zest, and juice until combined. Add the onion, celery, and whitefish and gently stir until combined. Season with salt and pepper. Cover and refrigerate for at least 1 hour and up to 24 hours before serving, topped with pickled onion.

PICKLED RED ONION
MAKES ABOUT 2 CUPS

1 cup red wine vinegar

¼ cup fresh lime juice

3 tablespoons sugar

1 tablespoon kosher salt

¼ teaspoon mustard seeds

¼ teaspoon coriander seeds

¼ teaspoon black peppercorns

1 medium red onion, halved and thinly sliced

1 // Combine the vinegar, lime juice, sugar, salt, mustard seeds, coriander seeds, and peppercorns in a small saucepan over high heat. Bring to a boil and cook until the sugar and salt are dissolved, about 1 minute. Remove from the heat and let cool for 5 minutes.

2 // Put the onion in a medium bowl, pour the vinegar mixture over, and toss to coat. Cover and refrigerate for at least 1 hour and up to 48 hours before serving.

MAPLE-MUSTARD-GLAZED CANADIAN BACON

SERVES 4 TO 6

The addition of three little ingredients—dark maple syrup, sharp Dijon mustard, and a smattering of black pepper—is all it takes to make a slice of Canadian bacon a crowd-pleasing, can't-stop-yourself-from-eating side dish.

⅓ cup pure grade B maple syrup

1 heaping tablespoon Dijon mustard

Pinch of freshly ground black pepper

1 pound sliced Canadian bacon

1 // Preheat the oven to 375°F. Line a baking sheet with parchment paper.

2 // Whisk together the syrup, mustard, and black pepper in a small bowl.

3 // Put the bacon on the baking sheet and bake for 6 minutes. Turn the bacon over, brush with some of the glaze, and continue baking until golden brown and slightly crisp, brushing once more with the glaze, about 7 minutes longer.

4 // Remove to a plate lined with paper towels. Serve warm.

SHAVED SMOKED PANCETTA

WITH BALSAMIC BROWN SUGAR

SERVES 4

Most pancetta is cured, not smoked, so this particular type is actually closer to the American bacon we grew up with—except that it is flavored with black pepper and other spices, leaner than its American counterpart, and fully cooked. Ask your butcher to shave it for you, as the way it crisps up in the oven, evenly coated in a sweetly tangy glaze of balsamic vinegar, brown sugar, and black pepper, is amazing.

⅓ cup balsamic vinegar

1 tablespoon light brown sugar

⅛ teaspoon freshly ground black pepper

½ pound very thinly sliced smoked pancetta

1 // Preheat the oven to 375°F.

2 // Mix together the vinegar, sugar, and pepper in a bowl until smooth.

3 // Lay out the pancetta in a single layer on a baking sheet and bake for 4 minutes. Turn over, brush with the balsamic mixture, and return to the oven. Bake until golden brown and crisp, about 5 minutes longer.

4 // Remove to a platter and serve warm.

HOMEMADE CHORIZO SAUSAGE

SERVES 4 TO 8; MAKES 8 PATTIES

There are lots of great prepared sausages on the market, but it can be fun to make your own for a change. And, despite how easy it is to accomplish, there is something about homemade sausage that sounds very impressive. This chorizo is smoky and garlicky and has just the right amount of heat. Of course, one of the other benefits to homemade sausage is being able to control those levels and adjust them to your personal taste.

3 tablespoons canola oil

1 small Spanish onion, finely diced

3 garlic cloves, finely chopped

2 teaspoons dried Mexican oregano

1 teaspoon ground cumin

1 teaspoon ground Spanish paprika

¼ teaspoon ground cinnamon

¼ teaspoon ground cayenne

¼ cup cider vinegar

1¼ pounds well-marbled ground pork shoulder

1 teaspoon kosher salt

¼ teaspoon freshly ground black pepper

1 // Heat 2 tablespoons of the oil in a small sauté pan over medium heat. Add the onion and cook until soft, about 5 minutes. Add the garlic and cook for 1 minute. Add the oregano, cumin, paprika, cinnamon, and cayenne and cook for 1 minute. Add the vinegar and cook until reduced by half, about 5 minutes.

2 // Remove from the heat. Transfer to a blender, add ¼ cup cold water, and blend until smooth. Pour into a bowl and let cool to room temperature.

3 // Add the ground pork to the spice mixture and gently mix to combine. Mix in the salt and pepper. Cover and refrigerate for at least 2 hours and up to 24 hours to allow the flavors to meld.

4 // To cook the chorizo, form into 8 patties. Heat the remaining 1 tablespoon canola oil in a cast-iron skillet over high heat until smoking. Add the sausage patties and cook until golden brown on both sides and just cooked through, about 5 minutes per side. Remove to a plate lined with paper towels to drain. Serve hot.

HOMEMADE BREAKFAST SAUSAGE PATTIES

SERVES 4 TO 8; MAKES 8 PATTIES

It can be tempting to stick with the familiar and easy option of picking up premade breakfast sausage, but try this homemade recipe instead; the results just might amaze you. Fresh, totally customizable to your family's taste, and completely recognizable, too, this sausage comes together so quickly you'll become a convert.

1 large or 2 small bay leaves

¼ teaspoon red pepper flakes

3 tablespoons finely chopped fresh sage

2 teaspoons finely chopped fresh thyme

2 teaspoons dry mustard

⅛ teaspoon freshly grated nutmeg

1 pound ground pork (about 70% lean) or ground turkey (90% lean)

2 teaspoons kosher salt

1½ teaspoons coarsely ground black pepper

2 tablespoons canola oil

1 // Using a spice grinder, grind the bay leaf and red pepper flakes to a fine powder. Add the sage, thyme, dry mustard, and nutmeg and pulse twice to combine.

2 // Combine the spice mixture with the ground pork in a large bowl along with the salt and pepper and mix with your hands until the spices are evenly dispersed throughout the meat. Cover and refrigerate for at least 1 hour and up to 12 hours to allow the flavors to meld.

3 // To cook the sausage, form the mixture into 8 patties. Make a small depression in the center of each patty with your thumb and forefinger. (This will help keep the patties flat as they cook.)

4 // Heat the oil in a cast-iron skillet over medium-high heat until it begins to shimmer. Cook the patties until golden brown on each side and just cooked through, about 5 minutes per side. Remove to a plate lined with paper towels to drain. Serve hot.

MENUS

LIKE CHOCOLATE FOR BRUNCH

UNDER THE TUSCAN SUN

NEW ENGLAND BED & BREAKFAST

SOUTHWEST BRUNCH

LE PETIT DEJEUNER

184 CROQUE MADAME

200 YOGURT CRÈME BRÛLÉE WITH FRESH FRUIT AND GRANOLA

45 LA FRAISE

SPA BRUNCH

139 SMOKED SALMON AND GREEN ONION SCRAMBLE WITH GOAT CHEESE BUTTER ON TOAST

210 GRAPEFRUIT SALAD WITH HONEY-MINT DRESSING

22 TEA LATTES

ALL-AMERICAN

74 CARROT CAKE PANCAKES WITH MAPLE–CREAM CHEESE DRIZZLE

249 HOMEMADE BREAKFAST SAUSAGE PATTIES

221 WILD MUSHROOM–YUKON GOLD HASH

32 BLOODY MARY BAR

OFF TO THE RACES

195 COUNTRY HAM AND FRIED EGG ON ANGEL BISCUITS

71 SILVER DOLLAR BUTTERMILK-PECAN PANCAKES WITH BOURBON MOLASSES BUTTER

28 BLACKBERRY-BOURBON ICED TEA

SOURCES

CAST-IRON PANS/GRILL PANS

Bobby Flay line at

www.kohls.com

KITCHEN GADGETS/UTENSILS

www.Cuisipro.com

www.Kitchenaid.com

CHEESES

www.murrayscheese.com

FRESH SEAFOOD

www.gortonsfreshseafood.com

KNIVES

www.kershawknives.com

POTS AND PANS

www.mauviel.com

TOMATO POWDER, VANILLA EXTRACT, VANILLA BEANS

www.thespicehouse.com

FISH, SHRIMP, MEAT, CHICKEN STOCKS

www.clubsauce.com

POMEGRANATE MOLASSES, SPICES, VANILLA BEANS, VANILLA EXTRACT

www.kalustyans.com

CUTTING BOARDS

www.johnboos.com

INDEX